HEA

Greg Forster is ...
Manchester. He studied classics, theology and social anthropology at Oxford, and is a member of the editorial board for Grove Ethical Studies, one of the Grove series of books which offer insight and analysis of contemporary issues from an evangelical standpoint.

Praise for Greg Forster's *Cohabitation and Marriage – A Pastoral Response*

'An excellent book on a timely issue . . . In its comprehensive grasp of all the social, historical, biblical and legal issues, this book provides a model of ethical thinking leading to practical conclusions . . . balanced and thought-provoking [it is] highly recommended to pastors grappling with the issues at the level of the local church as they affect ordinary people.' *Ministry Today*

'A worthy contribution to a rapidly growing literature on such issues.' *Church Times*

GREG FORSTER

Healing Love's Wounds

*A pastoral approach to divorce
and to remarriage*

Marshall Pickering
An Imprint of HarperCollinsPublishers

Marshall Pickering is an Imprint of
HarperCollins*Religious*
Part of HarperCollins*Publishers*
77–85 Fulham Palace Road, London W6 8JB

First published in Great Britain
in 1995 by Marshall Pickering

1 3 5 7 9 10 8 6 4 2

Copyright © 1995 Greg Forster

Greg Forster asserts the moral right to be
identified as the author of this work

A catalogue record for this book is
available from the British Library

ISBN 0 551 02949-8

Printed and bound in Great Britain by
HarperCollinsManufacturing Glasgow

CONDITIONS OF SALE
This book is sold subject to the condition that it
shall not, by way of trade or otherwise, be lent, re-sold,
hired out or otherwise circulated without the publisher's
prior consent in any form of binding or cover other
than that in which it is published and without a
similar condition including this condition being
imposed on the subsequent purchaser.

All rights reserved. No part of this publication may be
reproduced, stored in a retrieval system, or transmitted,
in any form or by any means, electronic, mechanical,
photocopying, recording or otherwise, without the prior
permission of the publishers.

CONTENTS

Introduction vii

1 Marriage and Remarriage – the present picture 1
2 Christian Ideals 23
3 Old Testament Divorce 39
4 New Testament – Marriage and Divorce 57
5 A Short History of Marriage and Divorce 85
6 Who Gets Hurt? 121
7 The Past and the Future – what is the good of divorce? 140
8 Pastoral Considerations 159

Appendix I
Henry VIII's Divorces 182

Appendix II
Prayers about Marriage and Divorce 185

Introduction

Two marriages out of three last, and the average length of a marriage is greater than it has ever been. In Britain, the marriage rate is higher than anywhere in Europe except Portugal, and remarriage is still attractive after the disruption of divorce. Yet the picture that is more frequently portrayed is one in which one marriage in three (or some such figure) will fail; divorce is on the increase, as is cohabitation before or instead of marriage; and the marriage rate itself is lower than it has been in over a century. The family is under threat, and marriage as we have known it is changing.

These are crude headline figures, and I shall attempt later to be more precise. They illustrate our ability to draw pessimistic conclusions when optimistic ones are just as valid – we see our cup as half empty, not half full. They also illustrate the way crude statistics can be misleading. In two reports covering the same twenty-year period, one gives a current marriage rate of eleven per thousand and the other thirty-six per thousand. Both are probably right, but one refers to the total population, which is ageing, and the other to those between (perhaps) eighteen and forty-nine who are not married. Neither report is clear, though both show marriage rates declining. We talk ourselves into a corner. We see morals (or at least stable life) under threat.

Such pessimism is not new. At the turn of the nineteenth century people saw the rising divorce rate as a threat to society – when perhaps 800 couples a year were divorced! *O tempora! O mores!* Since the Church has a historical and almost proprietorial interest in marriage its views and its practice are examined and have been reflected in the developments of divorce law in Britain over the past 150 years or so, if only by conscience clauses in the legislation. It still has a symbolic role, even where its precepts are ignored. Ministers of the Crown, some of them with divorces under their belts or married to divorcees, could object to the ordination of divorcees (or their spouses) as ministers of the established Church when the matter was brought before Parliament in the early 1990s on the grounds that it would set a poor example in society!

For ministers of the Church, and many followers of Christ, there is more than public example at stake. Large sections of the Church have regarded divorce, except perhaps in very limited circumstances, as a breach of Jesus' own commands and so as something with which they will not compromise. Among these people there will be some who have conscientiously stuck with a marriage that has been very difficult and failed to live up to its promise, and have refused to take an easy way out through divorce. Their interest in this stance is therefore not simply one of wishing to obey our Lord's commands, it is also a heartfelt and costly personal investment that they wish to see recognized and protected. If the Church seems to go back on its teaching about divorce, such people will feel as if they are themselves rejected and their sacrifice is spurned – in much the same way as divorcees have felt spurned over the past century or so. There are deep feelings on both sides, and a Church which takes seriously its Lord's pastoral heart must somehow try to express his fellow feeling with people on all sides.

Thus, though there may be one divorce law in England and Wales, and within it five 'facts' which may be used to demonstrate that a marriage has broken down irretrievably, there are also 160,000 or so reasons for divorce each year. Each case, and indeed each of the two parties in a marriage, has its own story, as do the many millions of marriages that do not break up each year and the 312,000 or so that begin. For each of us this is a personal story, as well as one with legal, social and ethical dimensions. For this reason I shall look at our Lord's pastoral practice with individuals as well as his moral teaching, and shall suggest that behind the teaching lie pastoral motives. It is not a strict legal pronouncement; there is a concern for personal justice rather than correct procedure. I shall also consider how the New Testament authors tried to apply Jesus' teaching to the new pastoral situations in which they found themselves, against different social backgrounds from that found by Jesus in largely Jewish Palestine. They, too, reveal the motives behind what they say, and those motives may teach us how to think about this issue. I shall also look at the historical development of divorce and the social setting of today's 160,000 divorces and 120,000 or so remarriages a year and suggest ways of applying the moral concerns of the Bible and Christian history with integrity in our own situation.

In this debate, integrity *is* needed. It would be easy for a couple wishing to marry after divorce, or for a Christian minister or a church organization wishing to keep in with the growing number of divorcees in society and in the Church itself, to find arguments to justify remarriage. Excuses can be found for conduct that is less than moral – whether the conduct be of those who petition for divorce, or the lawyers who push through that petition, or the church that will remarry the parties. The ethics can be bent for pragmatic purposes. Or is ethics a pragmatic discipline anyway, intended to sort out people's problems rather than condemn their sins? Some readers may feel that even by raising remarriage in church I am compromising my integrity and Christ's teaching, and by looking at the biblical teaching from an unexpected angle I am undermining the true Christian ethic. I am conscious of the danger, but am also aware of a betrayal of the other Christian principle of grace and forgiveness if I fail to ask such awkward questions.

I shall generally use the word 'remarriage' to mean marriage to a third party after divorce. This is convenient shorthand, though the word should strictly mean marriage to the same person. In some of the historical discussion, however, there is a further meaning, which will be plain by the context, of marriage after being widowed. Similarly, the word 'divorce' has changed its meaning over time, as I shall note in the appropriate section.

Divorce and remarriage are very much on the agenda today. This brings with it the danger that some of what I write will be dated soon after it is printed. For example, the Lord Chancellor recently published proposals for reforming English divorce law to encourage couples to work out their parting together, rather than fighting it out. He has been accused of seeking to save money rather than save marriages. Similarly, in 1994 the bishops of the Church of England were asked by its General Synod to reconsider remarriage in church – an issue that had been left in the air after a failed attempt to produce national guidelines in 1983. This issue will not go away, for with divorcees being involved in one-third of marriages in this country each year, clergy are repeatedly asked, with some hesitation, whether they 'do' the marriages of divorcees in their church. Even if the answer is no, that answer needs sensitive handling. Nor is it simply an issue for the Protestant churches. Of the 120,000 remarriages each year perhaps 1,000 will be in Roman Catholic churches, according to the Registrar General's figures. What he has recorded as a divorce, the Roman Church has adjudged to warrant annulment.

Divorce is not a brief event in the lives of two people conducted in solicitors' offices and perhaps a court. It is an ongoing relationship between those two people and their children, parents, second partners, and possibly their solicitors too; worked out in their homes or the parks and museums to which they take the children when it is 'their weekend', in their minds, and even in their churches. A pastoral approach to divorce and remarriage is not just an answer to the question 'Do you marry divorcees in your church?' It includes the issues of whether the Sunday School is geared to having half its members away with Dad every other week; how to handle the wedding where both sets of parents are divorced, and the bride's mother may expect to sit in the front row with her current partner while her 'ex' gives away the bride; and how to preach about Christian marriage in a church where half the members are divorced mothers left holding the baby – or the awkward teenager. It includes an awareness of the hurts and feelings and opportunities of a whole network of people in three or more generations for many years. A short book, written from limited experience, will not answer all such questions but I shall deal with some, and raise Christians' awareness of the others. In so doing I will reassert the message that God, and thus his Church, is interested in those who did not live happily ever after.

Finally, this is a book written out of the experience of discussing, arranging or refusing remarriages, and so draws on events in the lives of real people. It would be improper to discuss private affairs openly, so the case histories in this book are fictious in so far as names and precise details are concerned, but they are fact in that they draw on and amalgamate real incidents in real lives, and from published sources. I am grateful to those who have shared their observations of married life or recent events.

ONE

Marriage and Remarriage – the present picture

I answered the knock at the Rectory door to find a couple standing on the doorstep in the rain. 'Could we book an appointment to come and see you?' they asked hesitantly. 'It's about a wedding.'

'Would you like to talk now?' I replied. There was no urgency about what I was doing. As they settled in the study I checked that at least one of them did live within the parish – we have a pretty, mock-mediaeval church which can attract people from a wide area who have an eye to their wedding photographs. They named the road and I was satisfied that there were no complications on that front.

'There is one thing, though,' added the woman. 'My boyfriend's divorced. Does that matter?'

I stopped digging out the application forms and sat down. 'That depends,' I said, and began asking about the details.

One couple with their own story of sadness, love, hope and reconstruction – they are among a growing number who are aware of the Anglican Church's past reluctance to take the marriage services of divorcees. Yet they risk rebuttal none the less as they come to vicarage doors asking to meet. They have realized that there is a change in the Church's attitude, if only because of media reports about divorced parsons and debates in the General Synod. They wonder whether that change will benefit them. Some couples are only conscious of the pretty church backdrop (and perhaps the new permission from April 1995 for Registrars to use attractive buildings will relieve that pressure). Most will say that they want to 'do it properly' or that 'it doesn't feel right somehow' in a Register Office. Maybe that is as far as a generation that does not know how to use theological language can go towards saying they want God's support and blessing. Or maybe it is the way a culture that is not conscious of rites of passage voices its subconscious awareness of their value. They may hope that a church wedding will somehow help them get it right this time, especially if they merely went to the Register Office for the first wedding. Some, perhaps because they have Roman Catholic friends who were accused of 'living in sin' after a Registry wedding, wrongly think that the Anglican Church does not recognize a civil marriage as valid anyway. If one has not been married before she probably feels it unfair to be denied a 'proper' wedding, even if her fiancé is divorced.

Remarriages in Church – the statistics

A growing number of such couples have their requests granted in a free church or their parish church. In 1971 14,800 second marriages took place in a church (out of 84,000); in 1981 the figures were 23,300 out of 124,000; in 1986 27,300 out of 128,000; and in 1992 25,900 out of 113,000.[1] Some will say that they won't bother to marry if it can't be in church. That sounds like moral blackmail, but it is usually a genuine (though mistaken) feeling that a civil wedding is little different from cohabitation. It may not feel different but there are a whole range of legal benefits and securities that come with formal marriage, wherever it is entered into.[2]

In 1981, before the most recent round of discussions in the Church of England about remarriage in church, only 1,286 marriages took place in Anglican Churches in England and Wales in which one or both of the parties were divorced. In 221 of these both were divorcees.[3] Then debates in the General Synod led to a decision that, in principle, remarriage in some circumstances might take place in church. However the General Synod failed to produce an acceptable and workable scheme for regulating this. So, by 1991, the figure was 6,281 remarriages in

Anglican Churches[4] – an almost fivefold increase. Over the same period other Churches saw relatively little change. Remarriages in Roman churches rose from 991 (61 in which both parties had had legal divorces) to 1,185, an increase of one-fifth. Presumably that Church regarded the previous 'marriages' as null and had assessed that fact through their church courts. Remarriages in the various free churches fell by about 2,000, which may reflect the new Anglican willingness to take weddings which formerly ended up in the local Methodist or Reformed church. For comparison, in 1981 there were almost 352,000 marriages of which nearly 95,000 involved one or two divorced parties and nearly 180,000 took place in a church or synagogue. In 1991 the respective figures, again to the nearest thousand, were 307,000 marriages, 115,000 involving divorcees and 156,000 in church.

On a more local level, I have figures for my local Archdeaconry of 119 parishes between 1982 and 1993. In 1982 22 marriages out of the 1,241 conducted in those churches involved divorcees. By 1993 the number of marriages had declined to 814, but the number of those involving divorcees had risen to 119. The peak figure of divorcees marrying was 144 (out of 1,145) in 1989; and the trough figure for weddings was 753 in 1992, of which 96 involved divorcees. The general trend is down for total weddings and up for those involving divorcees.

Those 1,286 remarriages in Anglican churches in 1981 were legal. Strong moral pressure is applied to clergy not to take the marriages of divorcees but the Church authorities cannot override the legal capacity of clergy to officiate, so long as the proper processes are observed. I suspect that I was involved in one of the 1,286 for about then I was approached to take the wedding of a woman whose fiancé was divorced. It transpired that he had married at seventeen and that the relationship had broken down acrimoniously later the same day! He claimed that if the weather had been worse that morning he would not have bothered to turn up at the Register Office, and that when he did the couple had to round up two strangers off the street to act as witnesses.

Perhaps some of that story was about the wisdom of hindsight, but, to say the least, it indicates a severe lack of understanding of the nature of marriage. He continued to live at home and few if any of the neighbours knew of these events. By the time he got round to a formal ending of his non-existent marriage it was too late to seek annulment in the English legal sense, since non-consummation would have been difficult to prove and defective understanding or consent are not in themselves legal reasons to void a marriage. Nevertheless, it seemed appropriate to me then to regard the legal divorce as equivalent in moral terms to an annulment and to proceed with the marriage of a now wiser and more mature person.

This may seem an extreme case, and it is in that the marriage disintegrated within 24 hours, yet I have come across three similar cases in twenty-three years as an ordained minister. I do not simply mean instances where someone says 'I was too young', but occasions when the first days together shattered a relationship that had not been understood. For the record, one 'marriage' currently ends in a legal annulment for every 300 divorces.[5] In 1984, just before it became automatically possible to sue for divorce after one year's marriage, there were 1,036 applications and 871 grants of nullity. Subsequent figures are half this. This suggests that the more familiar and straightforward process of divorce is used to end marriages which merit annulment though the converse might have been true at one time. Annulment was used as a more rapid way of getting out of an uncomfortable marriage when the alternative was a three-year wait.

Factors leading to divorce: marrying young

Teenage marriages are one of the circumstances in which there is a significantly higher rate of divorce. This may be a reason for discouraging early marriage, though it is not always as simple as that. Sexual partnerships or cohabitations are likely without the formality of marriage, and they too will affect attitudes to marriage and its permanence. They may also leave scars which affect a person's ability to relate to another partner. The breakup of such relationships may merit as much pastoral support as a divorce, without its clear-cut character. Should a mother rejoice that her daughter's live-in boyfriend, of whom she never approved, has gone while the daughter laments her desertion? A teenager may rush into marriage (or, more probably in the 1990s, into cohabitation) as a means of escaping an oppressive situation at home with her parents. She may be carried away with the glamour of being a bride, and so becoming a person in her own right and not just someone else's daughter. The couple may well have a deep affection for each other which expresses itself in sexual and romantic love, and feel that they are mature enough to carry it through into married commitment. There is no reason, simply from the statistics, why they should be wrong in that belief. I have recently been involved in a golden wedding thanksgiving service for a couple who married at nineteen, while another teenage bride and groom whom I know have recently celebrated their diamond wedding. They have taken their vows seriously and worked at growing together. It must be said, of course, that they had more support from social attitudes in the 1930s and '40s than they might have now, but some of today's teenage spouses will look back on fifty years of such commitment, none the less.

It is a truism to say that all life is growth and change; that our perceptions and maturity develop not just through childhood but on into adulthood and old age. Such development, however, is particularly experienced in later teenage years and the early twenties. For a couple marrying during those years the danger of drifting apart rather than growing together is greater than for those who have developed more wisdom by the time they first meet and marry. Younger couples are not particularly conscious of that process as it is going on but think that they have achieved a greater maturity than perhaps they actually have. This may present a recipe for problems as the young couple grow older, though it is not a predetermined pattern. An older couple may be more set in their ways but have more life-skills with which to adapt.

One pattern which sometimes affects the divergence of couples as they grow older is the opportunity for adult education. It is not a new situation, though the circumstances imagined for Thomas Hardy's *Jude the Obscure* can hardly have been as common then (*c.* 1870) as now. A couple may get together as teenagers before either has had much education. The girl may well play down any academic abilities because she believes they do not attract her peer group of boys. Ten years on, the man may have had some training and be adept in his trade, if he has one; the wife, after some years of domestic responsibilities which in themselves add to her confidence, may nevertheless have no training in work-skills or other areas and be left behind by her husband's development. Or, she may find herself encouraged through their children's school to return to learning and ends up realizing a great deal of unfulfilled potential. Such changes in self-awareness, self-esteem and lifestyle are admirable, but they will place great demands on a relationship if one party's development does not match the other's. This, rather than simple immaturity or naïve expectations, may be the story behind the breakup of some teenage marriages. Marital breakdown among non-manual workers who married under the age of twenty is higher than among manual workers. The reverse is true among those who marry over the age of twenty.[6] I suspect that differences in subsequent education play a part in this.

Personal responsibility, social pressure

Marital instability is a product of the attitudes and behaviour of the couple themselves, and the choices they make about their relationship and activities. They are morally responsible individuals even if their actions may be immoral or irresponsible. But individual responsibility is not the whole of their story. We are all shaped by what we have seen in our own families and by what our friends and neighbours accept or expect. Judy

Wallerstein, in a seminal study of divorcing and divorced families in California,[7] found a high proportion of the children (particularly the girls) of divorced parents themselves ended up marrying early and divorcing after a short time. This was not so much the copying of a poor example as the results of an abortive attempt to find secure emotional support. However it is not a matter of shifting blame from the divorcing couple on to other individuals – their parents, perhaps. There are other examples which may equally influence one's attitude towards marriage and fidelity.

Two recent television advertisements depend for their impact on the innuendo of an extra-marital affair. In one, the husband drops off his wife and goes to collect a 'friend'. He then arrives with the female friend at a luxurious hotel . . . The dénouement is perfectly moral, however, as the wife reappears at the hotel for a surprise reunion with the long-lost friend and the husband drives off in the car (his real love, perhaps!). In the second, a man is invited by a sultry brunette to show her what his car can do. Their trip ends with a passionate embrace on the seashore before he drops her back where they met and then goes home. The dénouement again turns out to be morally proper, for when he asks his children where their mother is, the same brunette appears. The impact of these advertisements depends on the strong hint of sexual impropriety and marital unfaithfulness and it is that which, I suggest, will alter viewers' consciousness more forcefully than their endings. Even more seductive is the suggestion that for them all the car is the real love. Social attitudes are being remoulded by these and similar forces. This form of communication has more impact than the affirmation at a marriage service that the husband will 'keep himself wholly unto her so long as they both shall live', if only because such advertisements are continuously repeated on a day-to-day basis – unlike the marriage service.

Our moral choices are our own but they are shaped by the powers operating within society. In a book which discusses extra-marital affairs and how people may 'survive' them, Peggy

Vaughan suggests that it is not appropriate for the victims of affairs to blame themselves or their partners since the climate of society makes them happen.[8] (She claims, with reference to American behaviour, that 70 to 80 per cent of the population have had an affair.) She argues that the first way to survive a partner's affair is to move beyond personal blame. That approach to the problem is in itself an interesting and disturbing social fact. Vaughan is urging an ideology which sloughs off personal responsibility and blames something else outside our control. She is right – up to a point – to argue that individual behaviour is influenced by what goes on in the wider social world and needs to be understood, and maybe forgiven, within that context. She is profoundly wrong, however, in implying that an individual can be excused his actions if they go along with that social trend. Trends and statistics describe patterns of behaviour, they do not excuse or prescribe them nor do they explain them, except in so far as a copy-cat or snowball effect develops. On the contrary, the individual is morally free to respond to the trends around him.

More factors leading to divorce

Other factors which, in statistical terms at least, suggest a higher risk of divorce are pregnancy at the time of marriage, a previous divorce and prior cohabitation. The children of divorcees are also a vulnerable group. There may be overlap within these categories, of course. Cohabitants often delay a marriage until they are expecting a child, wishing to give their child greater security and legitimacy. Divorcees are also more likely to cohabit than those who have never married. Once again, however, much of significance lies behind the statistics, such as the couple's attitudes to marriage and, in the case of divorcees, the additional pressures they may face. One woman, Carole, whom I remarried told me afterwards that she had in fact been married twice before. The second of those marriages had been brief and very much a mistake, undertaken on the rebound from the first and under the influence of an exotic setting as much as love for the man. The third marriage seemed better thought through, despite some financial problems hanging over her as the result of children by the first husband.

Since 1971 the percentage of people divorcing who had previously been divorced has increased. In that year it was just under 9 per cent. By 1981 it was 17 per cent and by 1985, after the Matrimonial and Family Proceedings Act which allowed petition for divorce after one year, it had risen to 23 per cent. By 1989 the rise had levelled out, with just under 25 per cent of divorces involving a previous divorcee.[9] This seems a disquieting increase until we remember that the number of divorcees who are available to remarry, and so to divorce again, has risen steeply over the same period. During that time the remarriage of divorcees has risen from 15 per cent of all marriages to 34 per cent. Behind the statistics are not only the instability of second marriages and the unresolved weaknesses in those who have divorced, but also changing attitudes to the permanence or relevance of marriage which affects first and second marriages alike. This is supported by the divorce figures of those who have remarried after being widowed, whose previous experience of marriage was not distorted by divorce. As a whole, the divorce rate in this group is one-sixth that of first-time spouses. And yet among widows and widowers who married again in 1985–89 the rate of divorce is twice as high as among those who remarried between 1980–84.

A further factor which contributes to the instability of a second marriage is the presence of step-children. This factor does not appear as a statistic and may have varying significance in different settings. For example, one child may go round asking her mother's friends whether one of them will be her new daddy and obviously co-operate with the chosen man when a marriage takes place. The opposite scenario may also occur, where the children scheme together to wreck any new relationship by their parents and openly tell prospective partners of their intention. If such a relationship gets as far as marriage it has built-in problems quite apart from the attitudes or memories of the partners themselves. The children's motives may be an unrealistic hope that their parents will get together again; it may be a sense of loyalty to the non-resident parent; it may be their belief that the time and attention they have enjoyed with the resident parent will decrease or their own responsible role be overridden; it may be fear of more change; or it may be resentment at not knowing of the impending remarriage until late in the courtship. Such opposition may be found in adult children as well as dependents. Sometimes the children have not been brought into the developing relationship until late in the day or were not properly considered because they were resident with the other parent until they decided, as teenagers, that they did not want to stay there. In such circumstances a new spouse may be dismayed to discover a ready-made family with its own established patterns of behaviour. Conversely, a woman whose hysterectomy for cancer had deprived her of any hope of her own children may be overjoyed at her gift-family.[10]

If both parties to the new marriage have children there may be complications. The children may not get on with each other or resent newcomers in their house, even if their parents are happy together. Once again, such problems are not new. There is a story from the nineteenth century of parents (both of whom had been widowed) investigating a disturbance in the playroom. The wife comes out to announce, 'It is your children and my children arguing with our children.' It does need to be said, however, that some of these problems may well have occurred anyway between children and both natural parents together or between orphaned children and a step-parent. Conversely, wise step-parenting can actually benefit children, who may opt to take the new family name.

While marriage and divorce statistics do show the numbers of children caught up in divorce proceedings, they do not correlate divorces and resident step-families. In 1982 147,000 divorces were granted; 28.7 per cent of these involved childless couples. The remaining cases involved 158,000 children under sixteen and a further 68,000 over that age at the date the petition was filed. The comparable figures ten years later were 160,000 divorces, 168,000 under-sixteen-year-olds and 70,000 over sixteen. In addition, the age at which children suffer this loss has gone down. Of the under-sixteens in 1982, 27 per cent were under five and 32 per cent between eleven and fifteen. Those percentages were reversed ten years later to 32 per cent under five and 25 per cent in their younger teens. Census figures reveal the numbers of single-parent families and couples with dependent children but do not show whether those dependents are related by blood to both adults or only to one. Suzie Hayman, in *Other People's Children*, makes some rough calculations from figures that are available and concludes that 6 million people in Britain live in formalized step-families, which make up 8 per cent of existing households.[11] She adds that there are non-formal partnerships too, and suggests that up to 18 million people have some form of step-relationship, though it may only come into play perhaps once a fortnight.

The implication of these figures is that high proportions of children in, say, any secondary school class will be part of reordered families. A proportion of one in ten should not cause surprise, though it might cause alarm. Perhaps one in four might be more realistic in some areas. Therefore if a church school receives applications on the grounds that a child in a reordered family needs the moral support it can give, it should hardly discourage the request simply because it already has a high percentage of such families. They are part of normal society in the 1990s and beyond. Hayman cites the story of a child who went through school feeling the odd one out because of her mother's divorce and remarriage, only to discover in her final year that half her class had a similar experience. If membership of a church or Sunday School does not show such proportions, questions should be asked about the reasons. It may be that marriages of Christians are more stable than others, or it may be that divorcees feel excluded either by official Church pronouncements or by the awkward but well-intentioned questions that get asked.[12] The timing and planning of meetings or services could also sideline those with complicated stepfamily commitments.

A previous marriage, especially with children, may affect the second marriage in ways other than the complications between step-parents and step-children. It may have financial implications, either in terms of maintenance payments (or their non-payment), or because of disruptions in a person's career pattern while the first marriage was breaking up,[13] or because capital was disbursed when the first home was split up. A divorcee establishing a second home will be ten to fifteen years back down the mortgage ladder when he remarries. His income is split between two households if he is honest and responsible, or cannot disappear. Even if the income is adequate, his new marriage works on a lower standard of living than he and his wife might otherwise expect. As a result, he may take on more overtime or high-wage contract work that takes him out of the country and legitimately out of its tax system, further undermining his second marriage. If the second marriage was contracted before the final financial settlement of the first, he may find that the calculations on which he based his second household were mistaken and that he is living under far greater pressure than anticipated. The intervention of the Child Support Agency long after the original arrangements were made may further complicate this miscalculation. (I write this not to encourage financial irresponsibility or the avoidance of obligations, but to flesh out the statistics which point to higher divorce rates among those previously divorced.)

The higher rates may be due to personal inadequacy or ill-advised partnerships contracted out of loneliness, but there are other more mundane factors which make life harder second time around. We cannot argue that remarriage after divorce is wrong simply because its failure rate is higher than first marriages or remarriages after bereavement. On the individual level we can say that it ought not to be undertaken unadvisedly, lightly or without serious thought. However it is fair to ask whether steps on a national level to enforce responsible parenthood may in their turn disrupt and undermine sound family life in a second household. A society which accepts divorce on demand cannot avoid all corporate moral and financial responsibility for the results.

The third circumstance which appears to increase the risk of divorce is cohabitation prior to the marriage. A paper by John Haskey in the Office of Population Censuses and Surveys (OPCS) publication *Population Trends* both summarizes recent studies and produces data on this subject from the British General Household Survey of 1989.[14] He headlines his findings that of those who first married in the early 1980s, those who cohabited first were 50 per cent more likely to divorce after five years than those who did not, and 60 per cent more likely after ten years. There is a similar differential if separation without divorce (at the time of survey) is included in the figures. If, however, the length of the relationship rather than the length of the actual marriage is what is counted, then the differential drops. To use Haskey's example, if one counts fifteen years together before and after marriage, rather than fifteen years of legal marriage only, the added risk for ex-cohabitants drops to 20 per cent rather than 40 per cent. There is a similar differential between those using religious and civil forms of marriage. Greater stability seems to follow a religious ceremony. Haskey links this to family and communal support, and the effort and commitment invested in the marriage as well as to belief.

Haskey points out that a weaker attitude to the commitment of marriage allows cohabitation. Perhaps an uncertainty about the relationship in the first place led to a 'trial' union, and the uncertainty proved correct in the end. He notes also that those who have divorced might be more likely to register the cohabitation as something to regret or blame the other partner for, and so mention it to the researchers. The study did not consider the effects of cohabitation on the durability of second marriages, though a far higher proportion of those who have been divorced cohabit than of the bachelor and spinster population. Haskey's graphs show that in some age groups over 70 per cent of those who remarry cohabit first. A trial marriage is thus not an effective trial for marriage.

I have argued elsewhere that if cohabitation were given a more binding character in law this might have the educative function of stressing that walking away is not easy, as well as protecting cohabitants from exploitation.[15] Over 50 per cent of couples now cohabit before their marriage, though for some of them it is only during the last month or so, once the house is bought and its decoration is in progress. A further refinement in any detailed research in this area would be to determine any difference between long-term cohabitants and those who merely anticipate a marriage they have already arranged.

These statistics are based on a survey asking about cohabitation by a couple before they marry. It does not deal with cohabitation with another party, however. Such a relationship will have established emotional ties which have been broken, and may have created hurts and resentments which will lie dormant. If one of the reasons for unstable marriages is an attitude which regards commitment to a sexual partner as less than permanent and less than whole-hearted, then just like a previous marriage and divorce this may undermine the permanence of what appears to be a person's first marriage. If another of the reasons for unstable second marriages is the emotional baggage brought forward from the first, previous cohabitation will leave just as much disruption.

To complete this catalogue of woe, children whose parents divorced are more prone to divorce in their turn. Wallerstein noted that the daughters of such families particularly entered into marriage early and unadvisedly – perhaps looking for a male figure to look up to in the absence of their father – and that such marriages were vulnerable.[16] She draws attention, however, to the complexity of each person's situation, so that a simple 'search for a father figure' is not a total explanation of the problem. In the case she quotes an over-rigid access order by the courts contribute to her respondent's problems. A less-than-ideal pattern of adult relationships to learn from and copy also will not help a person's development from adolescence to adulthood and its relationships. A lack of emotional support in the formative years will leave a person less able to give emotional support to a spouse or children. (Such deficiencies are, of course, not restricted to a background of divorce.)

Wallerstein also points out that the situation is not deterministic. Many of her respondents dealt positively with the problems inherited from their parents' divorce. My own observations support that. People will speak of the unexpected long-term effects of being through their parents' divorce, and the grace of God to help overcome them. They show a sympathy for others and a concern for what is right that perhaps has grown out of an awareness of their own problems. Other researchers also back Wallerstein's observations, though other factors are relevant.[17]

Grounds for divorce

I looked at the decree. It gave the grounds for the divorce as irretrievable breakdown, of course, since this is the only reason now for divorce under English law, but then it amplified the reason. The fact on which the breakdown had been established was that George's conduct had been such that his ex-wife could not reasonably be expected to live with him. What conduct, I wondered, was so unreasonable as that? He mentioned a number of quite trivial things, which he was ready to admit that he had done, like occasional drinking or a short temper. What he objected to was the way the facts had been presented in her affidavit so that he seemed a habitual drunkard or a violent man. Grey areas in his life had been painted black. He had not wanted to oppose the divorce, but had been sickened by the way she had portrayed him.

When the Divorce Law Reform Act became law in 1971 the most common fact used to obtain a divorce was separation. Once the backlog of those who had been separated for two or five years worked through the system adultery became the most 'popular' fact. It still remains so in the case of petitions brought by the husband (running at just over 40 per cent). However, unreasonable behaviour has increased in 'popularity' whichever party is bringing the case. It now represents well over 50 per cent of the petitions filed by the wife and about 25 per cent of those brought by the husband, thus almost half of all cases. (Over two-thirds of divorce petitions are filed by the wife). Perhaps people's toleration of selfish behaviour has diminished over twenty years, or perhaps people are more unreasonable in their behaviour. More likely they, and their lawyers, have realized that no one will look too closely at the allegations made. Respondents are unlikely to contest a divorce, with the cost that entails. By far the cheapest way to divorce without the delay imposed by two- or five-year separation is to play up some quirk in one's partner's habits. This amounts to divorce by consent and as such it brings the law into disrepute since evidence is being contrived as blatantly as in the pre-1971 days of managed 'discoveries' in cheap hotel bedrooms. It also does nothing to restore harmony to the couple at a time when there might still be a *rapprochement*.[18] George's reaction to his ex-wife's accusations was typical: anger, a denial that his behaviour had been that bad, and a sense of injustice that anyone could actually believe her evidence. By the time he asked if I would conduct his second marriage a *rapprochement* was impossible. His ex-wife was living with another man and he was fairly certain that she had married him already. But he was still sensitive about any suggestion that his conduct had been seriously at fault and might need to be rethought.

Worse or better?

It is often claimed that the number of divorces, and thus the divorce rate, is rising. While this is correct – there are about twice as many divorces per year as there were just after the Divorce Reform Act of 1969 – the picture is more complex. The rate rose steeply in the ten years after that Act from 6 divorces per thousand extant marriages in 1971 to just short of 12 per thousand in 1981. Thereafter it has fluctuated near that level and currently stands at 13.7 per thousand (1992 figures). The raw figures grew by 99 per cent between 1971 and 1980, but only by 5 per cent between 1981 and 1990 – less than 1 per cent per annum. The rise in the rate per thousand is partly due to the decline in the number of marriages taking place and thus the number of married couples 'available' for divorce.

Wallerstein also notes a steep rise in her Californian figures in the 1970s and a stabilization in the 1980s (p. 345). She also reports a conversation with the anthropologist Margaret Mead, who suggested that in no previous society had there been experience of such free terminability of marriage and lack of communal pressure on couples to stay together.[19] (It might be fairer to say that we have no detailed record of such a society. It might even be so dysfunctional as not to survive very long, though I wonder whether some aspects of urban and slave society in the Roman Empire might fit Mead's description.) If this assertion is so, perhaps the current stabilization of the divorce rate indicates the sort of equilibrium such a society will find, in which affective marriage – i.e. marriages arranged by the affection and courtship of the parties concerned – is followed by a high initial failure rate and a long-term, cumulative failure rate of about 25 per cent (based on Haskey's graph). If there is any good news in that possibility, it is that things have stopped getting worse. The figures do not, however, indicate those broken relationships which involved deep emotional commitment through cohabitation, but never got as far as marriage so do not have the benefit of just dissolution through divorce.

As those who are left grow old

Andrew left Helen and almost immediately moved in with an already separated colleague from his works, leaving Helen with the children. Though she resisted the idea at first, a divorce eventually went through, leaving the children in her custody and him paying maintenance. He enjoyed a fair amount of freedom with his new partner, a dual-income-almost-no-kids type of lifestyle. Helen, however, was tied to the children who were young at the time. Five years later he had remarried while she remained alone. Perhaps her attitude made her an unattractive companion, though her sense of duty to their sons was admirable. It did limit her free time and leisure activities, however, so that her circle of friends was restricted.

Divorce does offer some chance of a just settlement of a couple's affairs if they split up. However, that does not remove the deep-seated element of injustice in divorce. It may be a relief from one particular set of unpleasant circumstances, but it often opens the door on a wider pattern of unfairness, which is the result of individual choices and responses but also reveals injustice on a wider social level.

If the rates of remarriage of men and of women are compared we find that divorced men are twice as likely to remarry in any one year as women: just under 4.5 per cent of eligible men but just under 2 per cent of eligible women in 1992. Consistently, more men remarry than women. In raw figures the imbalance is not so great, with 78,000 men remarrying in 1982 as against 74,000 women, but over the years this inequality has built up so that Helen's circumstances are common (even though up to 60 per cent of divorcees might expect to form a new relationship within five or six years of the breakup). Like so many others she is literally left holding the baby, with its attendant limitations. I felt angry for her since she was imprisoned by her social circumstances. I was indignant, as she was, with Andrew for his treatment of her. I was at times exasperated with her, since she had dug some of the hole she was in herself, despite her Christian beliefs.

Liam has a different story. If Helen's tale is of how a woman can find herself manoeuvred into protracted singleness by the way men behave, his is the reverse. He is very bitter about his ex-wife, though he would love to reconnect with his son who is now his only surviving blood relation. However, mother and son moved following a slum clearance and he has lost contact. He vows he will never remarry, though he is an attractive enough character in many respects. He feels he could never trust a woman again. Perhaps he is wrong to generalize from his experience of one woman, but his reaction is not uncommon. He lives alone and smokes too much so that his general health is declining. He has signs of high blood pressure but has no one to encourage him to see the doctor. From time to time he is to be found in church.

Again, Liam's situation is a mixture of his own and his ex-wife's making, and yet he is by no means alone in his isolation. There is a social dimension to his plight. If twice as high a proportion of divorced men remarry than divorced women, it is not just that all such men find greater liberty in making new friendships. Those who do not make a new partnership are at significantly higher risk of premature death than those who do, and also compared to the general population. Though divorced women are also more at risk than the general population, it is divorced men on their own whose risk is greater still. A higher proportion of the surviving men remarry in part because the base number of surviving divorced men is lower. It may seem grandiose to talk about these greater risks in terms of social justice rather than individuals' inhumanity to each other, but I am drawing my evidence from a study written largely because a Government Green Paper on *The Health of the Nation* appeared totally to have overlooked the role of marital status in supporting or undermining people's health.[20] Such an oversight perpetuates, and even perpetrates, the injustice.

In conclusion

This chapter can only be a partial picture of the sociology of divorce and remarriage. It is a picture that Christians have until recently been reluctant to look at, except in terms of discussion as to whether it is right to remarry *them*. We are perhaps realizing that some of *them* are *us*, and that *they* represent a fair proportion of our parishioners if not our congregations. Pastoral concern for divorcees will not be limited to whether we are able to remarry them, though the spin-off from that debate may effect the notice the Church receives. Divorce and remarriage are personal facts. There are, however, issues of wider, social justice at stake as well as personal behaviour and morals.

Notes

1. These figures, relating to England and Wales, come from *An Honourable Estate* (London: Church House Publishing, 1988), p. 49, (GS 801) quoting data from the Office of Population Censuses and Surveys (OPCS). The table does not state whether the remarriages of widows and widowers are included, which were about 25 per cent of the total of all remarriages in church or Register Office in 1971, but only 5.5 per cent in 1986. 1992 figures come from OPCS *Marriage and Divorce Statistics 1992*, (London: HMSO, 1994).
2. I have discussed the matter more fully in *Cohabitation and Marriage* (London: Marshall Pickering, 1994).
3. *An Honourable Estate*, op. cit., p. 57, reproducing data from OPCS.
4. The 1991 figures come from OPCS, *Marriage and Divorce Statistics 1991* (London: HMSO, 1993).
5. *Ibid.*
6. K. Dunnell for OPCS, *Family Formation 1976* (London: HMSO, 1979) pp. 36f.
7. J. S. Wallerstein and S. Blakeslee, *Second Chances* (London: Corgi, 1989), pp. 207, 341, 345.

8. P. Vaughan, *The Monogamy Myth* (London: Thorsons, 1991).
9. OPCS, *Social Trends 21* (London: HMSO, 1991), p. 40.
10. These examples are culled from Suzie Hayman, *Other People's Children* (London: Penguin, 1994), as well as my own observations.
11. *Ibid.*, pp. 4, 5.
12. Paula Clifford, *Divorced Christians and the Love of God* (London: SPCK, 1987), cites the times she or others in her situation have been asked thoughtlessly, 'What does your husband do?'
13. Christopher Compston, *Recovering from Divorce*, (London: Hodder and Stoughton, 1993), p. 44, suggests a divorce can set a professional back ten years. This is probably exaggerated, but the point is well made.
14. John Haskey, 'Pre-marital Cohabitation and the Probability of Subsequent Divorce: Analyses using new data from the General Household Survey', *Population Trends 68* (London: HMSO, 1992), pp. 10ff.
15. *Cohabitation and Marriage*, *op. cit.* Figures derived from the OPCS *Marriage and Divorce Statistics 1992* (London: HMSO, 1994).
16. Wallerstein and Blakeslee, *op. cit.*, pp. 207, 340ff.
17. J. Dominian et al., *Marital Breakdown and the Health of the Nation* (London: One Plus One, 1991), p. 26, cite evidence. Kuh and McLean suggest a 40 per cent greater likelihood of divorce for people whose parents divorced. Not all the problem here is emotional. Divorce has the effect of reducing the standard of living, particularly for the wife and children resident with her. Lower living standards are themselves conducive to divorce or separation.
18. The Lord Chancellor's recent Green Paper, *Looking to the Future*, (London: HMSO, Cm2424 1993), para. 5.6 makes this last point forcibly: 'Allegations over behaviour require the recollection of things best left forgotten.' He is more reticent than I am in suggesting the lawyers' hands in the

manipulation of facts to be proven.
19. Wallerstein and Blakeslee, *op. cit.*, p. 339.
20. *Marital Breakdown and the Health of the Nation*, op. cit., pp. 1, 2, 19ff., referring to the Department of Health Green Paper of 1991.

TWO

Christian Ideals

'Are you going to obey him?' I asked, grinning.

She pouted and he chipped in, 'She doesn't obey me now!' Sarah and James had been living together for a couple of years already so that was a fair comment.

'Ooh, no,' she affirmed, and looked across at him. 'We have talked about that, haven't we?' He nodded.

Of all the supposed Christian ideals in marriage the wife's promise to obey is perhaps the one that has been established most firmly in folklore, unless the belief that somewhere in the service someone should say 'I do' is a Christian ideal. Both, in their way, are erroneous. 'I do' is part of the American ceremony as seen on TV; 'obey' is part of a mutual bargain, in Ephesians at least, to be subject to each other's best interests. I tried to explain this while assuring Sarah that I would not make her say something she did not want to. In the end we left it that she would not say it in the service. A habit built up over a couple of years is not going to be changed by one word in the wedding service, though from time to time a bride will shrug and say, 'OK, go on then, I'll say it.'

More concerned to stress the husband's part of that bargain, I did my best to help James see how loving Sarah in the self-giving way that Christ loved his people might work in their relationship, both now and when they were married. Since both were working, how much of the housework did he take on, I wondered. 'He's a great cook,' she volunteered. 'I never do anything when we have friends round.'

What was the ideal which had drawn them to want to marry in church? What is 'Christian marriage', and how does it differ from the folklore or the alternative on offer at the local Register Office or nearby stately home? Was it just a matter of the location and grander ceremonial? Was it the high ideal of companionship within the covenant that the couple make with each other? Was it the sacramental permanence and portrait of God-like love which attracted them? It was hardly the earthy honesty which speaks of the joy of the bodily union they already knew, nor the austere asceticism which in the past saw marriage as a protection against the lusts of the flesh. Were there features of the Christian message that are to be seen in marriage, or even in the trusting companionship that they already knew but which they would not have recognized without some prompting? In the first flush of romance it is not the done thing to think about things which might need forgiveness, though in practice they must have been learning about it through their relationship. These features are all part of the ideal in Christian marriage. Like the hologram pictures on some bank cards, they are there but not always seen together or in the same light.

This multi-dimensional picture is rich and should be held up to couples – those considering marriage, those caught up in cohabitation, those already committed in marriage, and those whose previous experience of marriage is better portrayed by the austere flip-side of the card – flat, black and white, and bedeviled with legal small print. But it is not merely an ideal to hold up for admiration, nor to turn away from sorrowing. It presents us with a measure against which each relationship can be tested and so is a template by which each can be shaped. However, it is not a rigid straightjacket, it is multi-dimensional. The Christian ideal contains the promise of grace to live up to it, for it is offered to us by God as a destination to choose and work towards rather than as a mirage to tease. The most significant part of the Anglican marriage services is the blessing that comes after the promises. This is not because a priestly blessing makes the marriage, but because its message is that *God is backing you*.

He wants your marriage to go well. All the promises that his grace guides us morally and enables us to understand, forgive and grow in maturity, are true in your marriage as is the assurance that even failure holds within it the seeds of restoration.

This is what I tell all the Sarahs and Jameses who come to me for a church wedding, but it had taken on a particular poignancy when Sarah was filling in the original application form. 'What do I put here?' she asked, pointing to the box which gives the alternatives spinster/widow. She had been married before and, from her hesitancy as I asked about it, it had been a painful time. It was not that she tried to hide the past, but it was difficult to talk about it. James's gentle support as we talked suggested that his love had offered her restoration and a growing self-confidence. Recent writing about the benefits of Christian marriage has stressed this enriching feature, to the extent that in the *New Dictionary of Christian Ethics and Pastoral Theology* G. C. Meilaender can speak of 'the healing purpose of marriage' as one of its traditional three 'goods'.[1] Earlier generations would not have spoken in such terms, but used the phrase 'remedy against sin'. Given a conviction that Christianity is about acceptance and forgiveness, I believe it is right to work towards fuller healing and greater renewal. The 'unforgivable sin' of the gospels is not divorce but a refusal to recognize that the Holy Spirit can work in this way and so not to allow him to do so. I did not go into all this theology with Sarah, but her relief and delight when I agreed to take the wedding was obvious. For her it was not just that the venue would be right for photographs. It was another small acceptance of her, despite what had gone wrong for her in the past.

Three good things and true

So, what are the characteristics of 'Christian' marriage which we uphold for people to make their own? The features which I mentioned above have, in one generation or another, been highlighted by Christian teachers. Some of them may seem to twentieth-century Christians to be strange versions, or even distortions, of the truth. Perhaps that is because we notice the highlights and forget what is behind them. What follows is not a full attempt to describe the development of Christian ideas about marriage, it is more like a series of still photographs, picking out significant points in a film. Chapter 4 covers more of this story.

Children and their care

Augustine (c. 354–430 AD), writing in the dying years of the Roman Empire, held that the procreation of children was the great purpose of marriage, one of the 'goods' that lay at its heart. He saw in Genesis 1:28 the divine words to be fruitful and multiply as the first command (and also the first blessing) to humankind. He also felt the anxiety of his class at the time – that there should be children to carry forward the family name, to pray at the family mausoleum (with pagan or Christian prayers), and to maintain the Roman tradition. This view of child-rearing was coloured by a Christian ideal that children might be born who should be born again to the greater glory of God through the faith.[2] These ideals of fertility and faith are reflected in the Anglican marriage services.

But Augustine did rise above the limited anxieties of his time. Secular Rome set so great a store on child-bearing that the failure to produce a child might be grounds for divorce. Augustine rejected the argument. The oath (*sacramentum*) of marriage forged a permanent bond which could not be set aside.[3] 'Even for the sake of offspring,' he writes, 'the marriage bond is not broken but remarriage remains adultery.'[4] The inability to have children is not a reason to dissolve marriage (though the deliberate intention to avoid children or the refusal to consummate the marriage may be reasons for nullity in Roman canon law and modern secular laws).

Unless there is some medical reason for restraint I believe children should be part of a couple's plans, though there is a good case for deferring child-bearing to give them time to know each other better as husband and wife. Some want to wait until they can afford it. That is likely to be never! A decision not to have children should be confident enough to survive a lonely old age. It is important for a couple to accept that if the plans do not work out and children are born unexpectedly, it is the children and not the plans who are important. Such thinking about plans over children would have seemed strange to Augustine, and his attitude lies behind the present official Roman stance on contraception. In *De Bono Conjugale* (I.v.) Augustine writes that sexual intercourse with a paramour with the sole intent of having children is morally better than intercourse with one's spouse within marriage simply for lust's sake.

Augustine had been a teacher of philosophy before his conversion and that background merges with his Christian faith in his thinking about sexual relations. Classical philosophers regarded it as evil to have lost rational control of one's self and so come under the domination of the material world. For them passion was the great evil, meaning not simply emotions such as anger or love but irrational actions or feelings in which the self comes to be controlled by the force of such emotions. The words *passio* and *pathos* have the basic meaning of suffering – being on the receiving end and thus losing control. This thinking found echoes in Christian denunciation of the flesh. The writers of the New Testament letters had denounced the lust and sexual immorality which they noted around them. To them such conduct would not lead anyone into the kingdom of God. They were conscious too of an imminent tribulation and subsequent return of the Lord. Paul suggested that marriage itself might distract from the business of Christian life and service. Though he recognized the potency of human sexuality it sounded somewhat grudging when he wrote that it was better to marry than to burn! (1 Corinthians 7:9).

Later generations of Christians read this caution about marriage in the light of the obvious evils of lust in late Roman civilization rather than in the light of Christ's return. They understood that Paul, in 1 Thessalonians 4:4 had been talking about taking a wife (*skeuos* – 'vessel') without lust rather than about a man's sexual self-control generally.[5] Celibacy became an end in itself to avoid contamination as much as a freedom by which someone was enabled to serve the kingdom of God more wholeheartedly. Augustine wrote that the better Christians a married couple were, the sooner in their married life they would begin to refrain from sexual intercourse with each other. He also speculated whether in an unfallen world procreation would have been possible without intercourse.[6] His argument is complex because of his consciousness of original sin. The Pelagians accused him of treating God's good gifts as evil. Looking back on the debate he seems to have come within a whisker of such a statement. 'All that comes of intercourse is lust.' He has exaggerated out of a desire to demonstrate that humankind is not now free to determine its own good conduct, but is depraved and needs God's grace to achieve even the good things of marriage.[7] Taken out of this polemical context Augustine's support for marriage seems grudging and his arguments forced. But he was aware from his own personal past that sexual drives could hold people in thrall, and that lack of self-control could be destructive.

Loyal support

The second 'good' Augustine saw in marriage was *fides* – often rendered 'fidelity' but having a wider meaning, covering loyal relationship. He knew that this natural benefit was admired among pagans and was a basic building-block for society at large. For Christians subject to the dangers of lust, marriage offered protection against that evil and fidelity within it gave grounds for security. We might find here the roots of the idea expressed in modern pastoral theology by the word 'covenant'. But if challenged, Augustine would have denied that a man could find in marriage the comradeship that he would expect with a like-minded male friend. Given the lack of education among women of the upper classes among whom Augustine grew up this is perhaps understandable as an observation rather than as a declaration of principle (though in his mother he had reason to know otherwise).

He spoke of the *fides* of chastity and how the carnal and youthful temptations to incontinence might be brought through it to honest use in the begetting of children, and the glowing pleasure of seeing children grow so that out of the evil of lust the marriage union may bring forth some good. For Augustine, marriage exists where there is a willingness for intercourse and the rearing of children, and for a lifelong association. The fact that it might not exist where such will is lacking is no grounds for dissolving a marriage. As Augustine goes on to speak about the *sacramentum* of marriage he makes it clear that for Christians even separation does not void that bond.

Augustine continues with points that seem strange to twentieth-century readers but which should make us pause before we idolize either marriage or sexual expression of any friendship. Marriage is good and remains so even if abstinence is better. It is good not for its own sake but because by the propagation of humankind it enhances the opportunities for fellowship and friendship. Clearly these relationships are higher in his thinking. If our priorities are better we need to know why.

Support against sin

Thinking about this particular 'good' of marriage was developed further in terms of 'protection from sin'. By Thomas Cranmer's time (1489–1556) marriage could be spoken of as a 'remedy against sin, to avoid fornication'. It is easy to smile at this language and the fifth-century fears behind it. We lack the healthy dread of sin that our ancestors had, and our Western image of sexual love is distorted more by Marie Stopes and *Playboy* than by fear of Mani or Pelagius! Many Christians cherish the frank delight expressed in Genesis 2:23 ('At last, bone of my bones . . .' – someone I can get on with!) or the love poetry of the Song of Songs. We play down the dire warnings of Ephesians 5:3ff. A modern vicar promoting a Christian view of marriage will quote American surveys that suggest loyally monogamous couples have the best sex, rather than stating that the better they are, the sooner they give up sexual relations in

CHRISTIAN IDEALS 29

marriage![8] Even the ASB marriage service seems to contradict Cranmer by speaking of the 'joy of their bodily union'.

Before we laugh at Cranmer's austerity we should learn from it. A remedy against sin is no light blessing. To write off the sexuality God gives us as lust, and to see all passion (in the ancient or modern sense) as improper, is excessive. Yet it is moral sense to recognize the dynamic of sexual appetites, and that feelings alone do not justify an action or relationship. There is a great deal of selfishness, self-gratification and inhuman treatment of other people that goes on under the fair-sounding guise of love or freedom or self-discovery. We deceive ourselves if we think otherwise. Humankind can be most inhumane. Marriage is an institution which functions to restrain such abuses. Mutual and exclusive trust, expressed through explicit consent and vouched for by witnesses, is the proper setting within which sexuality should be enjoyed, and is a gift of freedom and security. It allows opportunities for self-giving love which may not find their fullest and richest expression in haste or uncertainty; without it, the restraints on selfishness are minimal. In this sense marriage offers a remedy against sin, though the cure is not automatic. We have to choose to take the medicine.

We can extend what we understand by 'a remedy against sin' beyond that. We are not dealing just with sexual sins such as adultery or promiscuity. There are also sins of exploitation and abuse between people. Feminist writers claim that the institution of marriage itself enslaves women, at times keeping them under the control of father or husband and offering them no other trade than housewifery.[9] They rightly show the abuses, which formed the background to the divorce law reform debate of the nineteenth century. But they overlook the restraint which marriage and its restriction of dismissal at will imposes on casual male domination. The second and third-century Church used its moral influence with its members to make them treat the marriage bond as secure, even for the powerless ones in their society. In a different setting such security became a prison. The nineteenth-century reforms in Britain removed some of the rigidity from the roles expected of husband and wife and forced each to meet the other on more individual terms. They removed the exploitation which was built into the law and in so doing remedied a different injustice. In that, they enabled the Christian ideal of mutual respect and edification in love. However, as expectations change and roles are less certain there is now scope for new instability and for different forms of exploitation. One form of structural sin may be remedied, but another – an almost casual ease in casting off old spouses – has replaced it. Freedom without an internalized moral framework opens the way for a different bondage.

The feminist writer Liz Hodgkinson, who suggested that 'as marriage laws have become more codified women have lost all their rights', also confessed that since the beginnings of sexual liberation in the 1920s women have become even more imprisoned.[10] 'What really needs to be changed,' she goes on, 'is the way in which men and women see each other. They must stop regarding each other as possessions, accept each other as individuals, and let each other remain so.' For her, non-intimate friendships, like brother and sister, are the pattern for the future. There is a right place for brother/sister-like relationships, but sexual attraction and bonding are strong, however, and what Christians offer is not its rejection as exploitative. Some may lay it aside, as they feel a deeper calling to celibate service, but for most the way should be the hallowing of the bonds forged out of sexual love so that they do not lead to exploitation.

Literature put out by a lesbian centre in Manchester consists of 'testimonies' by women who meet there. Perhaps for diplomatic reasons they say little about their sexual self-expression, but what struck me about their stories was how they each had found friendships in which they were respected as people and not exploited by dominant or insensitive male partners. I believe that the kind of relationship which they yearned for, and which Hodgkinson suggests forms the needed change, is contained in the picture of marriage upheld by St Paul in Ephesians 4 and 5.

Between them those two chapters emphasize the growth to maturity which Christians want to see in each other as they imitate Christ.

Commitment

The third of Augustine's benefits speaks of marriage as a *sacramentum* – a soldier's oath of allegiance to his general, validated and hallowed by imprecation to the gods and not to be broken. The stress in Augustine's teaching was on the holy bond that cannot be dissolved by human whim or action. While he sees the other two 'goods' of marriage as part of the common experience of humankind, this third he regards as peculiar to the people of God, sanctified as much by their baptism as by separate promises before the Church. In *De Nuptiis et Concupiscentia* (I.xvii.) he argues that neither divorce nor the adultery which perhaps preceded it actually break the bond of marriage. For him, even the 'Matthean exception' (see p. 62) left a bond, even if a legal divorce did take place; and the 'Pauline privilege' is merely that for a wife to be put away by a pagan husband is not in itself a sin (see p. 75ff.). The marriage bond was not loosed even if the purpose for which marriage exists – the procreation of children – was frustrated.[11]

In Roman law, consent was the key feature of marriage, though because of the nature of Roman society consent was at times lightly given and lightly taken back. By classing consent with an oath of allegiance it was given a degree of certainty, reinforced by the communal authority of the Church, which it had previously lacked. At that time the word for 'consent' or 'intention' was *affectio*. In the Middle Ages a subtle change was introduced by means of the double sense of that word so that 'affection' as well as 'intention' (both *affectio*) came to be seen as a central 'good' in marriage. Cranmer chose as his third purpose, for which matrimony was ordained, not sacramental permanence as such but 'mutual society . . . in prosperity and adversity'. The permanence is physical rather than metaphysical. He writes of a quality of relationship which represents the divine commitment to humankind but it is seen in practical terms in the commitment of the couple, whether their life together is hard or easy.

Anglican services retain the neat liturgical pattern of these three 'causes for which matrimony was ordained,' but they have been adapted considerably. 'Mutual society, help and comfort' have become the practical expression of the *sacramentum*. Those words have been adapted further in the modern services to be the first rather than the last of the 'good things' of marriage, and include again the idea of faithful commitment. This change of order reflects the changing emphasis in marriage. Bearing and caring for children remains a primary 'good', but loyalty as a remedy against sexual sin has been transmuted – first into the hallowing and right direction of the God-given sexual instincts, and most recently to the delight and tenderness of bodily union seen as enhancing the couple's personal and emotional union. This delight in sexuality, even if it is seen as part of a fuller personal unity, is a far cry from Augustine's almost grudging recognition that sexual love was a part of marriage so long as it was not engaged in out of lust. The undertones brought into the service by modern thinking about romantic love also rearrange what we see in it, as 'affection', in the modern individual and emotional sense, can drown the major theme which is moral commitment.

To love and cherish

Love in marriage is not a modern idea. Cranmer asked the couple, 'Wilt thou . . . love, honour and keep . . . ?' and this reflected St Paul's teaching in Ephesians. But the understanding put on 'love' by those who speak the promises is modern. We seem to be speaking of romantic, emotional or even sexual love as the words trip off the tongue. It is right that those feelings should be celebrated. It would be impossible to exclude them, given the images woven round the marriage day in magazines, stories and gossip. Yet in an age when permanence and commitment seem to be dirty words in many areas of life the couple should realize that their promise to love is a moral commitment, given in response to a command. It is an act of their moral faculties, their will, not a biochemical response. It is not a description of their current feelings projected into the future. They say 'I will', meaning 'I am committing myself to that.' Marriage is not an excuse for the care and respect which is expressed in the romance of courtship to cease.[12]

When St Paul told husbands to love their wives he used the standard Christian word for love, *agape*. In non-Church Greek it is a rare word, with the connotation of caring concern. That was what the Church meant when it spoke of love and that is what should be seen in Christian married love too, alongside the other elements of emotion and sexuality. It is a moral quality as well as a romantic one; it is a conscious and deliberate choice. Thus when the couple respond 'I will', they are not just saying 'That is what I am going to do.' It is a moral commitment which will continue through all the seasons of life, in sickness as in health, and not merely while the feeling lasts. To gloss the phrase 'till death us do part' as meaning the death of the marriage or the death of love distorts the promise. It may be realistic – the moral strength to keep the vow may fail – but that is not what the words mean. The promise is to act caringly, even if the emotions are drained by crying children or time's grim tentacles. Love involves duty as well as feeling in a dutiless world.

If Sarah had understood that first time round, she had been let down as her husband lost himself in clubs and among his male circle of friends. I had seen from the way she described it that it still drained her to talk about the way it sapped her self-esteem. James showed his support then, and his presence had brought reassurance and confidence to her again, but their two years together had not been easy. Perhaps her second attempt at marriage could be dismissed as grasping for a lifebelt in a storm. Maybe it was breaking all the rules – they were living together unmarried, and she had been married before with her former partner still living. Yet their relationship showed something of that healing purpose of marriage by which some modern writers have reinterpreted the 'remedy against sin' as sexual drives being redirected along wholesome channels. Dare I suggest that it was even an antidote to the effects of the sins of others? It is risqué to justify a breach of Christ's explicit instructions by an appeal to the apparent work of his healing Spirit. The danger of failure may be twice as great as for those who do not already have a failed marriage behind them. But where all hope of rebuilding the first marriage is gone, 'she is not enslaved' to it (1 Corinthians 7:15). Given that the Gospel is about forgiveness and renewal it is appropriate to forget what lies behind (except to learn from it) and to press forward towards that renewal.

I have already suggested that any couple may learn something about mutual forgiveness in their relationship even before marriage, and also, that what Paul wrote about married love in Ephesians 5 should be seen in the light of what he says about Christian life as a whole in Ephesians 4:15–32. Loving honesty can enable us to grow towards maturity and true maturity is found in the imitation of Christ. Perhaps marriage – even a second marriage – is in that sense sacramental: it can demonstrate the God-like qualities of acceptance and tolerant understanding. But it does not happen automatically. Not every relationship works that way. But we can draw on the graces of forgiveness and patient love – and a Christian will do that consciously – in order that the natural good of marriage may be enriched and preserved. The pattern of the service becomes a message. Daunting promises are followed by the assurance of God's support in words of blessing, after which the couple move forward to the communion rail to pray, symbolizing their need for God's grace to support their promises.

Christian marriage

The lifestyle in marriage which Christianity offers to couples is one of permanent security and support 'till death do us part'. Someone coming for a second marriage will probably have thought that through and may want it more intensely than someone coming first time round. This does not in itself justify remarriage, but I have more hope for the Sarahs and Jameses of this world who are prepared to talk over their hopes and fears than for the couple who thought 'preparation for marriage' meant handing in a list of hymns and leaving. To speak of Christian marriage as a lifestyle is to stress its moral nature. It is something we opt for and ask God to help us with, even if we have to come back to him many times. It remains as the ideal even if someone does not opt for it. Now that marriage has become an affective relationship between two people rather than an institution with relatively fixed roles, the affirmation 'I will' in the service needs to be understood more fully as 'I will work with you to make a go of it together', or better, 'I will, the Lord being my helper!' The couple should also consider whether they can see that commitment as their vocation in life, to which God has called them, as the 1928 Anglican service suggests.

In the marriage service the declaration that the couple are married is set beside the challenge 'Those whom God has joined together, let no man put asunder.' Jesus did not direct these words at divorce courts. Divorce was then a matter for the husband and courts did not enter into the situation. It is more like those letters which begin, 'To whom it may concern'. Today the couple themselves are being told not to break up their own relationship; their families are being warned not to disrupt the marriage and to accept the couple's right to cleave together as their primary relationship; friends and future acquaintances are being warned off – these two belong together, let no one come between them by seduction or slander. In due course their own children too must learn that their parents have to have time and space for each other, whatever their parallel duty to their offspring. (When there are step-children involved in a second marriage, their feelings and needs have to be worked through, too.)

Christians offer this pattern of marriage to couples for their own good – for God's commands and patterns are intended as benefits for humankind. When it is set out as an ideal it does not describe failure and divorce, so that these possibilities have often been discounted in considerations of Christian marriage. There have been times and places where an appearance of conformity to this standard has been maintained by society. Perhaps Britain in the early years of this century was one such place, which is why calls for 'traditional values in marriage' have a certain appeal (however even then there were moralists voicing their age-old cry that morals were getting worse). The Christian ideal also gives us a yardstick against which marriage as an institution, and our individual marriages, may be measured.[13] That all marriages – even the 'good' ones and the first-time ones – fall short of the ideal is a cause not for despair but for renewed commitment.

Notes

1. G. C. Meilaender, 'Sexuality', in *New Dictionary of Christian Ethics and Pastoral Theology*, eds D. J. Atkinson and D. H. Field (Leicester: InterVarsity Press, 1994), p. 75.
2. Augustine, *De Nuptiis et Concupiscentia*, I.iv.ff., I.xvii.
3. *Ibid.*, I.x.
4. Augustine, *De Bono Conjugale*, I.vii.
5. Cf. Augustine, *De Nuptiis et Concupiscentia*, I.iv. I have discussed this text in detail in *Marriage Before Marriage?* (Nottingham: Grove Books, 1988), p. 5. The normal meaning of *skeuos* is 'baggage', which corresponds to a rabbinic idiom for 'the wife' (English slang is no kinder: cf. our 'the old bag'). But, given Paul's respect for women, it is better taken to mean that each man should control 'his (sexual) equipment'!
6. *De Bono Conjugale*, I.i., iii.
7. *De Nuptiis et Concupiscentia*, I.x., I.xvii.
8. The Revd. David Holloway, speaking on the radio in early 1995, also reported in the *Church of England Newspaper* (13 January 1995).

9. Cicely Hamilton, in 1909, cited by Liz Hodgkinson, *Unholy Matrimony* (London: Columbus Books, 1988), p. 93.
10. *Ibid.*, p. 100.
11. *De Bono Conjugale*, I.xxiv. Augustine draws a parallel with the indelibility he saw in priestly orders, which remained even if there was no congregation or a man had been disbarred from exercising priestly duties for misconduct.
12. The idea of developing in love through the stages of life is discussed, for instance, by Jack Dominian, *Marriage, Faith and Love*, (London: Darton, Longman and Todd, 1981).
13. This approach is explored in relation to marriage and to cohabitation by Gary Jenkins, *Cohabitation: A Biblical Perspective*, (Nottingham: Grove Books, 1992). I have covered similar ground to the material in this chapter in *Cohabitation and Marriage* (London: Marshall Pickering, 1994).

THREE

Old Testament Divorce

It is natural that Christians should look to the Bible for their ideals of marriage and their reaction to divorce, as well as considering traditional and contemporary reactions to it. We cannot simply ask, 'What does the Bible say?' We cannot simply look into a concordance to find references to 'divorce', and then analyse the meaning of those references without first asking a few basic questions. For example, did the word 'divorce' have the same connotations for the biblical writers as it does today for us? What kind of society was it in which the process described as divorce took place? Also, particularly where moral teaching is being given by the prophets, apostles, and by Jesus himself, we should ask not only *what* was said but attempt to see *why* it was said. Motives and principles may be as important in applying such teaching in our changed social setting as the actual words themselves. Relevant texts will include those where the English text does not use the word 'divorce' but where the Hebrew or Greek uses a term which is elsewhere translated 'divorce'. Consider this passage which brings out the vigour and implicit violence of the Hebrew words for divorce. Standard translations use the words 'cast out' and 'send away'.

> So she [Sarah] said to Abraham, 'Divorce [*gareš*] this slave-girl...' And God said to him, 'Don't be displeased for the sake of the lad and your slave-girl; obey everything Sarah says...' So he woke early in the morning, took bread and a skin of water, gave them to the slave-girl. And the lad he put on her shoulder, [he gave her custody of the lad?] and divorced [*šilleh*] her, and she went away and wandered the wilderness of Beersheba. (Genesis 21:10ff.)

This is the other side of the marriage of Abraham to Sarah, which is rightly upheld as an example of loyalty in the face of adversity and disappointment. I would not wish to reject or undermine that picture, but there is another side to the life of a man who was not a twentieth-century (AD!) monogamist. Hagar, the slave-girl, is given to Abraham as his 'wife', in Genesis 16:3. Because Ishmael, Hagar and Abraham's son, is also involved in the expulsion, the word 'divorce' sits uneasily with modern readers of this passage. But the words *gareš* and especially *šilleh* are the normal words for 'divorce' elsewhere. They are intense words, both using the form of the verb in Hebrew which denotes vigorous action. In addition, the phrase 'the lad he put on her shoulder' is difficult since Ishmael was more than sixteen years old as the text now stands! Some modern commentators see signs of multiple sources being merged inexpertly by an editor (whom they elsewhere describe as a genius). I suggest that it is an idiom reflecting a custom corresponding to our award of custody (cf. Isaiah 9:6), irrespective of the age of the lad. Later she exercises the father's prerogative of arranging his marriage. There is no mention of any 'bill of divorce', but at that point in history (*c.* 2000 BC) that is hardly surprising. What Abraham does put into Hagar's hand are clear tokens that she is being sent away – a *viaticum* of bread and water.[1] Hagar sets off for Egypt, her native land. She has to find support – or die. Divorce was a violent act, though Hagar's need to leave a close-knit Bedu tribe exaggerated the fact.

On one level, this story illustrates for us the meaning of 'divorce' in Israelite culture. It was no long, drawn-out legal process in impartial courts. The final decision was rapid, and in the hands of one of the parties to the relationship. There are other cultural differences which bear upon any application we may wish to make of this story to our own circumstances – not least the place of Hagar as a subordinate wife in a polygynous household. As such Hagar might have expected her position to be secure, and Abraham's initial reluctance to divorce her corroborates this.[2] However it should not be taken as a model for action and was probably never intended as such, even when it was a 'new' story. Then, on a second level, it explained relationships between Israel and neighbouring tribes – Ishmael's descendants – and their relative places in God's scheme as Israel saw things.

On a third level, it is the story of God's dealings with *a* man – admittedly a special man within his scheme for his chosen people, but a story of a man who did not always get things right either by the standards of his day or those of later periods in Israel's moral development. Its prime aim is not to tell the story of a divorce, but the story of a longed-for heir. I believe, however, that as the first listeners recalled their ancestor's exploits they would identify with his story – like father, like children! He was a friend of God, the *nabi* (a prophet or holy man), to whom God would listen; he was the joker, who made good even when he got into terrible scrapes and with whom God would work against the odds. His story (which includes Hagar's story) is one in which God's 'Plan A' is revised to 'Plan B' and then 'Plan C' as God adapts to Abraham's misplaced attempts at co-operation and their consequences.

Plan A concerns Sarah and Abraham and does not include Hagar. However when Sarah's faith in her ability to bear the promised heir fails, she and Abraham take the initiative and, in line with accepted custom at the time, she gives him her personal servant as a wife (Genesis 16:1ff). Not surprisingly, this leads to jealousy and Hagar, by now expecting a child, takes flight. God's Plan B begins to take effect as she is sent back with a promise of great things for her son (Genesis 16:7ff). In due time Plan A comes to fruition and Isaac is born, but with his weaning a couple of years later the tensions within the household come to a head as Ishmael is caught teasing the toddler (Genesis 21:8ff). Abraham's first thought is his paternal loyalty to Ishmael and his obligations under current custom to Hagar. It takes divine prompting as well as wifely nagging for him to go against those duties. (For those who might think nowadays that divine prompting will permit them to act how *they* wish, it was only after Abraham had tried to keep his obligations that God directed him otherwise.) So, Abraham drives out Hagar as the only way to avoid ongoing conflict that would damage both children and all the adult parties involved. God's Plan C comes into operation as he supports the divorced woman and keeps his promise to her and Ishmael, even if it is now separate from his links with Abraham.

If the first listeners could identify with the story, so may we. God worked with the consequences of actions which were and are morally questionable and kept faith with people even when they got into a moral or emotional mess, adapting his relationship with them to the new circumstances. We cannot, with twentieth-century tints to our spectacles, say that it was all right for Abraham to get rid of Hagar because he should not have committed polygamy in the first place. However he did, and took on obligations to her which were recognized in his day (cf. Jacob and his wives' maids, Genesis 30:1ff.) and which the storyteller recounts without criticism (though there is a hint that Abraham's lack of faith is criticized). We live – and God lives – with the consequences of our actions. Nor can we say that Abraham was a special case, despite the significance of this incident within salvation-history upon which St Paul was to build in Galatians 4:21ff. Abraham is significant in the story of our salvation precisely because he is an individual who kept faith with God, and with whom God kept faith, despite moral failures. He is the father, the role-model of faith for us. That does not make moral failure such as the complex web of errors which often builds up to a divorce right, let alone something to be encouraged. It does assure us that it does not rule us out of God's plan or the community of God's people.

Deuteronomy – divorce assumed?

Discussion of divorce in the Old Testament is not limited to the narrative sections. We find it in the history of the returned exiles and in the lived-out parable of Hosea's marriage and the denunciations of Malachi. However before all that it figures in the case-law of Deuteronomy.

Despite the assumption made in the Pharisees' challenge to Jesus over divorce – reported in Mark 10 and based on the opening verses of Deuteronomy 24 – there is no formal legislation *for* divorce in the Old Testament. There are two passages where it is explicitly forbidden in certain circumstances, namely when a man has been compelled to marry a woman whom he had forced, and when he has made a false accusation against her soon after their marriage that she had not come to him as a virgin. Then there is Deuteronomy 24, in which a restriction is placed upon remarriage after divorce. In these passages the availability of divorce – to the husband – was assumed, and we can deduce, as the Pharisees did, that certain procedures were to be followed, such as the issuance of a formal 'bill of divorce'. This bill of divorce was a protection for the wife, who could not then be accused of bigamy if she married another man. (Polyandry was never acceptable to the Israelites, though polygyny was.) The need to put the divorce in writing gave added protection, since it prevented the husband uttering words of severance in the heat of an argument. To get it down in writing would take time, and we may conjecture that at the time the legislation of Deuteronomy was enacted there would be the problem of finding a scribe to do the writing. A further check on a husband's precipitate action might be the terms of the marriage compact between him and his bride's family. Fifth century BCE Jewish papyri from southern Egypt (and the far later rabbinic material) refer to repayment of a dowry in the event of early death or unwarranted divorce.[3]

The Rabbinic descriptions of the divorce process show the requirement of a formal delivery of the written document, which had to be correctly dated before witnesses. The Samaritans may have also required reference to their high priest. How early these Rabbinic provisions applied we cannot judge. Isaiah 50 and Jeremiah show knowledge of the written bill and the legislation of Deuteronomy 24 in the sixth century BC. It would be reasonable to assume that the involvement of witnesses came before the writing of a document. I suggested above that the food for her journey which Hagar was given was a symbol of the separation. What is implied in the provision of Deuteronomy 24, however, is that divorce could be enacted by the husband without recourse to any higher authority, though he could not simply act in the heat of the moment.

A final point, implied in the provision of Deuteronomy 24 and made explicit in both Samaritan and Jewish sources, is that the divorce left the wife free to accept marriage to another. Indeed, given the cultural and economic circumstances of Israel at the time when Deuteronomy was written down, it is difficult to imagine anything other than this. To think that remarriage was discouraged and that there were many women alone in their fathers' houses is a very twentieth-century interpretation of Israelite literature. What Deuteronomy 24 makes clear (and Jeremiah 3 confirms) is that it was considered abominable and forbidden for a man to remarry his earlier wife after she had married a second man.

How frequent was divorce in Old Testament times? That is really several questions since it relates to a thousand-year period and there is very little evidence, none of it explicit. At times, notably when Malachi prophesied, it was sufficiently the abuse of the age for him to put some effort into denouncing it. For other periods, we simply do not know. Some may be right in arguing that as the wisdom literature does not mention it and offer advice about it, it was not very prevalent. But does the gap in the wisdom literature prove that? Until perhaps ten years ago there were very few practical books of advice on Christian bookshelves on how to cope with divorce – at a time when the divorce rate in England and Wales was running at about 150,000 a year. Before then the standard advice (as in Proverbs) was not to get into that situation. If you did, you were on your own!

What we can say about divorce during the Old Testament periods is that it was sufficiently common for it to be used as a very vivid parable in the prophetic literature to illustrate God's despair and (sometimes ambivalent) hope of reconciliation with Israel. Also, it was common enough (as was marriage itself!) for there to be no need in the law books for the normal divorce procedure to be spelled out. It is only specific limitations to the general practice that are discussed in the Law. In addition, the Jewish community in southern Egypt (which was admittedly not orthodox by later standards) was quite familiar with it. On the other hand, it is only at the time of Malachi that the abuse of divorce becomes so prevalent that a prophet is moved to denounce it. Or is this the case? Is it perhaps only Malachi who has the sensitivity to see things from the woman's point of view, and challenge the male assumption that the wife of one's youth is expendable? His unique use of a word for 'companion', to which we shall return later, may suggest this angle in his perception of things. In considering these texts and letting them speak to us, we need to be aware of the blinkers worn by those who wrote them and allow them, in God's name, to remove the twentieth-century moral blinkers that we wear.

The text of Deuteronomy 24

We turn, then, to what Deuteronomy 24:1–4 has to say in detail. The Authorized Version is wrong in not recognizing that all the clauses up to verse 4 are conditional. There is no instruction to divorce the wife in verse 1b. It may be translated thus:

1. Suppose a man takes a woman and marries her; this is the procedure if she does not find acceptance in his opinion because he finds in her some obscenity of a thing,* and *if* he writes for her a severance† document, and he delivers it into her hand and divorces‡ her from his house,
2. and *if* she goes away from his house and makes her way to another man,
3. and *if* the second husband dislikes her, and writes for her a severance document and delivers it into her hand and divorces her from his house,

or suppose the second husband who took her for himself as his wife dies,
4. *then* the original husband who divorced her is not permitted *at all* to change his mind§ and take her to himself as his wife, after she has been defiled,"

since that is an abomination in the Lord's presence and you (thou) are not to cause guilt to the land which the Lord your God grants you as heritage.

I have used italics to indicate words not in the Hebrew but included to clarify the sequence of dependent and dominant clauses. This and other translations in this chapter are my own – to highlight (perhaps inelegantly) important nuances. Some of them are:

* *'erwat-dabar*. An almost unique phrase, which in Deuteronomy 23:14 refers to decency in using the camp latrines! The word *erwah* means 'nakedness', particularly sexually explicit nakedness, which for the Israelites was a thing of shame.
† This word, usually rendered simply 'divorce', comes from a root (CRT) which means 'cut' or 'chop down' – again the language is of a violent act.
‡ Literally, 'sends her out', but the word has a technical sense, even without 'from his house'.
§ The RSV renders this word simply 'again', but it is surely stronger than that. It is the normal word for 'turn again' and 'repent'.
" Again, a unique usage. It could be reflexive – she has defiled herself, or the very rare verb form could have the force of a definite passive – she has been defiled (by someone else).

The Rabbinic debate, which forms the background to Mark 10 and its parallels, was on the meaning of the phrase 'obscenity of a thing'. The school of Shammai held it meant adultery (though in the Mosaic law adultery was a capital offence) or some serious sexual impropriety. The more libertarian school of Hillel allowed even bad cooking as a reason for divorce! A generation later Aqiba picked on 'in his opinion (in his eyes)' to justify divorce on the grounds that the man found someone who looked prettier. In view of the connotations of the word *'erwah*, it would seem that it was Shammai who had grasped the original intention of Deuteronomy rightly; that it was for sexual impropriety of some sort that the Law expected divorces to be initiated. That being said, the reference to a captive wife in Deuteronomy 21:14, which insists that the woman be respected as a person in her own right, reckons on divorce simply because 'you have no delight in her', i.e. sexually or personally the man has lost interest. In either case, however, what we have in Deuteronomy is permissive legislation by implication rather than a command to divorce such as the Pharisees seem to have read (according to Matthew 19:7) in these words.

I have included the note above about the word 'again' or 'change his mind' partly in response to Andrew Cornes' emphasis in his discussion in *Divorce and Remarriage* on the desirability of reconciliation, based largely on his interpretation of the image of the marriage of Yahweh and Israel, and Yahweh's summons to Israel to return.[4] I share Cornes' longing to see sound reconciliation between a separating or divorced couple but believe that this particular text is quite strong in forbidding the man to go back on his action. Jeremiah, in quoting this passage (3:1–5), makes a play on the word 'return', thus I am not inclined to take it as a mere idiomatic phrase meaning 'again'. Why should it be so abominable for this particular reconciliation to take place? Why does it pollute The Land and offend the Lord?

In verse 4 we are told that it is because 'she has been defiled'. It is easy to ask, *'What* has defiled her?' Is it her conduct prior to the dissolution of the first marriage? Since the second marriage is not precluded by this conduct this seems unlikely. Is it the second marriage in itself? Since it is only remarriage to her first husband that is abominable and not, it would seem, a third marriage to a fourth party, Cornes is probably right to reject this view. He then suggests that the reason is that the second marriage is to count in the first husband's eyes as adultery, which *he* cannot countenance or seem to condone, whatever the Law may allow. This avoids the logical inconsistencies of the first two ideas. It may also, in a very tentative way, anticipate what Jesus says about a second marriage being tantamount to adultery. It does, however, suffer from the drawback of seeing pollution in the land as depending very much on the individual viewpoint of one husband. It is, as Cornes admits, an elusive understanding of the text, for all that it has the backing of the great S. R. Driver.

May I put forward a further possibility? It may seem equally elusive and might be dismissed as a twentieth-century angle on the text, but I shall defend it in context. I start from the word 'she has been defiled'. This is one word in Hebrew and is, in the precise form used, unique in the Bible. In Hebrew, verbs have a variety of forms which indicate not only the action itself but also its mood or intensity. This form could be reflexive – she has defiled herself. However, the particular form used is rarer and not a normal reflexive. It has a more passive tone to it. In that case it means 'she has been defiled by someone else'. I say 'by someone' because I think the right question to ask is not '*What* has defiled her?' as S. R. Driver and others have done, but '*Who* has defiled her?' I suspect that that is a more Israelite question, since Israelite Law is more concerned with broken personal relationships (with God or with people) than with abstract offences.

So who has defiled her? Was it herself, in her conduct before the dissolution of the first marriage, or in contracting the second marriage? Was it her second husband, in marrying her? (It was presumably not in *his* divorcing her, since the text allows for his death – which also militates against the suggestion made both by Atkinson[5] and Harvey[6] that the original context was a prohibition of wife swapping. The arguments quoted above weigh against these possibilities, and the rare form of the verb also implies that it was not her own actions. By whom, then, was she defiled? I suggest that it was the first husband himself who was responsible, and for this reason he cannot go back on his actions. Maybe R. Aqiba was right in emphasizing the phrase 'in his opinion', even if his use of the phrase was flawed. It was in the first husband's *opinion* that the woman found no favour or acceptance. She did not agree with his assessment, and her father's house (we may suppose) challenged his view but could not prevent the divorce. Her name was blackened and she was treated as a chattel. The first husband cannot now say, 'I didn't mean it, it doesn't matter, you can come back now.' *That* would be an abomination in the Lord's presence, after he has driven her into the arms of another man. He cannot treat her as dirt and then act as if it did not matter.

All too easily we assume that it was the woman who was to blame, and much interpretation of the passage has gone along with that assumption. Perhaps Deuteronomy is taking the woman's side. This view also could be seen as an anticipation of Jesus' teaching. It may seem that this is a very twentieth-century – even feminist – approach to a text which was never interpreted so in antiquity. One may counter by pointing out that it proved difficult to interpret in antiquity, and those who attempted to do so made their own very chauvinist assumptions which equally may not have been the original writer's intention.

We have already seen how the captive wife (in Deuteronomy 21) is to be treated in a humane way and not used as a mere chattel. She, of all people, was in a vulnerable situation, a captive with no family to enforce her case. Yet the Law is on her side and protects her from the unjust whims of her captor husband. If such an attitude is found in one section of Deuteronomy, might it not be implied in another? Similarly, the falsely accused bride has the Law's protection against her husband's change of mind. Most commentators do see in all these passages, and the customs that lie behind them, restrictions on the man's freedom to divorce and incentives to think twice before taking precipitate action to dissolve his marriage. The socially weak woman, open to exploitation or abuse, receives protection from the Law.

Malachi – 'I hate divorce'

In Malachi 2 we find the other major section of teaching on divorce. Unfortunately, this also contains difficulties in interpreting the text. Some commentators suggest that those who copied the text distorted its original meaning because it seemed to conflict with the permission to divorce they saw in Deuteronomy, and the custom which they knew and perhaps practised. The situation is further complicated by the relation of this passage to the accounts in Ezra and Nehemiah of Jews' marriages to foreign wives and their subsequent expulsion or divorce (Ezra 9–10; Nehemiah 13:23–31). Though there is no date given in Malachi's text for his ministry, the reference in 2:11 and the tradition that he was last of the prophets suggests that his work is close in time to that of Ezra and Nehemiah – possibly soon before it. Malachi implies that Jewish wives have been divorced in order that younger, foreign wives may be taken (or may take precedence in the formerly polygynous household). Neither Ezra nor Nehemiah add this complication to their picture. Their complaint is not with the divorce of Jewish wives but with the introduction of non-Jewish culture, language or belief. What Malachi would have thought about Ezra's solution – the divorce, in God's name, of about 120 non-Jewish wives – we do not know. Nehemiah seems to have been content with exacting an oath that the practice should not be perpetuated.

The relevant text in Malachi 2 may be translated as follows:

10. Surely we all have one Father, surely one God created us? For what reason do we each deal treacherously with our brother, so as to violate the covenant of our fathers?
11. Judah has played traitor and committed abominable acts in [Israel and] Jerusalem, for Judah has violated the holy place* of the Lord who loves,† and married the daughter of an alien god.
12. May the Lord deprive‡ the man who dares to do this of any witness or spokesman or intercessor with the Lord of Hosts from among the tents of Jacob.

13. And this other thing you get up to – covering the Lord's altar with tears, weeping and groaning. He still refuses to turn towards the offering to accept it gladly from your hands.
14. So you go on saying, 'Why?' Because the Lord gives evidence between you and the wife you married young, whom you – yes you – have betrayed, and she it is who is your comrade,§ the wife to whom you pledged your troth.
15.‖ And did he not make *us* one and bequeath spirit to *us*? And what is the oneness looking for? – godly descendants. So take [ye] care of your spirits, and no betrayal of the wife you (thou) married young.
16. for 'there is a hatred of divorce,' says the Lord the God of Israel, 'and covering one's robe with violence,'¶ says the Lord of Hosts.

Some of the more important nuances of this text include:

* Perhaps 'place' is the wrong noun to supply here. '. . . trespassed upon the Lord's holiness' may get the force of it.
† There is no object for the verb 'love', and it is not clear what is its subject. The sense could be 'which he loves' (i.e. the place), or 'whom he loves' (i.e. Judah loves God) or most likely, it seems to me, 'who loves him' (i.e. God loves Judah).
‡ There may be a pun here, since Malachi's verb is the root that supplies the noun for a bill of 'severance' or 'divorce'.
§ This word is unique as a feminine noun, though its masculine form implies the comradeship of men together, in a club or regiment. Has Malachi coined the usage to make his point?
‖ This verse is a mess, perhaps because copyists baulked at his words (though what they have made of it does not make sense), or perhaps because Malachi was stumbling over himself in his enthusiasm for the point and the play on words between the one God and the one flesh union of Genesis 2. It could be rendered (with slightly different corrections): 'And the One God made her, and bequeathed his spirit *to her. And what did the One look for? godly descendants, and He will*

keep them with his Spirit, and let him not betray the wife you married young!'

¶ For 'there is a hatred' the usual translation is 'I hate', which is no doubt the sense. The Hebrew as it now stands is more impersonal and so, perhaps, more intensely implacable. It is there, as an objective fact. The word for 'violence' often carries connotations of male violence or violence against a woman. We have already noted how the word for 'divorce' itself is a word of intense action.

It would seem that the specific pattern of behaviour that Malachi is denouncing is the divorce of older wives – who have grown old with husbands to whom they were married when both were young – probably in favour of younger women. He regards this as an act of violence, even if it has been carried out according to customary process. After a relatively long period of marriage, and perhaps the death of the wife's father, she and her brothers would be in a weak position as far as recovering the dowry or hindering the divorce were concerned. An additional slap in the face for these Jewish women (and their Jewish families), born of the same heritage as their husbands, was probably that the new young wives were not Jews and their religion and lifestyle were alien. (Nehemiah 13:24 brings this out in his description of the problem.) Perhaps the new young wives and their families had pressured for the divorce of the senior wives, who would otherwise have exercised greater influence in the household which could, in theory, have remained polygynous. If Nehemiah and Ezra can be used to set the social scene of the ills Malachi was denouncing, even men of power in the Jewish community, who should have known better, were acting in this way.[7]

We may conclude by noting two points. While the hatred for divorce is not qualified or narrowed down the specific context was probably as indicated above, and was in Malachi's eyes – and God's – tantamount to a violent abuse of power against weaker members of society. Such concern is also shown later in the book (3:5). Secondly, while the Hebrew text is difficult, it does seem that Malachi is harking back not to the Law but to the pattern of creation as portrayed in Genesis 2, where husband and wife are to be 'one flesh'.[8]

In examining both Deuteronomy and Malachi I have tried to bring out not just the letter of the text but also the spirit that lies behind it. In both, the motive for what is said seems to be the protection of the weak and the prevention of abuse of the power that came to men simply by their being male in that society. In Deuteronomy we are dealing with case-law, the underlying logic being 'Be sympathetic with the underdog, because you too have suffered and God cared enough to redeem you.' This comes out in the distinctive Deuteronomic version of the Sabbath commandment (5:15). Malachi's prophecy is concerned with the honour of God, and he is appealing to the character of God as revealed in creation to support his argument.

Hosea – be like God!

Hosea found his painful marriage to be a prophetic sign of God's persistent love for Israel, and was perhaps the first to speak of God as the husband of his people (or at least the first to redeem such imagery from the excesses of Canaanite paganism). Just as God continued to bother with Israel despite her unfaithfulness, so Hosea continued to bother with Gomer. He never actually divorced her, although her adultery would have justified such action in the eyes of his contemporaries. (Strictly speaking, her behaviour invited the death penalty under the Mosaic law.) His redemption of her from slavery mirrors God's willingness to take back wayward Israel; it reflects God's forgiveness and desire for reconciliation. Hosea lives out the principle of the Law that Israel has forgotten – to imitate God. In doing so he perhaps sets an example of searching for reconciliation in troubled marriages, but it is not an example that he consciously teaches in his prophecy. His overriding theme was that Israel should undergo a general moral and sexual reformation and return to her true God.

Supporting marriage – commands and provisions

There are many places in the Old Testament where the good of marriage is affirmed, notably in Proverbs 31 (seen from the husband's point of view!) and 19:14; (but look also at v. 13!); in Psalms 45 (a royal marriage) and 127; and in Genesis 1 and 2 (to which I shall return affirming God's blessing and human delight). There are also numerous passages where marriage-breaking is condemned, not least in the seventh and tenth commandments and again in Proverbs 6:25–35 and 9:13–18 (again from the male viewpoint).

One feature of Old Testament legislation is worth a special note. It comes in Deuteronomy 24:5:

> Suppose a man has taken a new wife; let him not go out with the host nor undertake any business. He shall be at liberty at home for one year to enjoy himself with his wife whom he has taken.

The motive for this provision is given simply as the happiness of the couple (or at least the husband!). We might also ask whether the importance of raising children – for his family's name and the establishment of his place in the land – or the fear that intercourse might contaminate the army engaged in a holy war were in mind here. It might even be that astute commanders did not want troops whose minds were elsewhere. The claims of the state upon the couple were also restricted for their first year as the importance of establishing the family unit was recognized.[9] Whilst there may be many advantages implicit in this passage, the main motive put forward does appear to be for the good of the marriage.

Notes

1. There is no need to suppose with von Rad (*Genesis*, London: SCM Press, ET² 1963, p. 228) that this was a pitifully inadequate supply. In 1948 Wilfred Thesiger, with local Arab guides, set off across the empty quarter of Arabia – a far less hospitable country than the Negev – with little more by way of provisions. Little else will keep!
2. Cf. K. A. Kitchen, *The Bible in its World* (Exeter: Paternoster Press, 1977).
3. Cowley, *Jewish Documents of the Time of Ezra* (London: SPCK, 1919, p. 45ff., Cf. also 'Gittin' in *The Mishnah*, H. Danby, trans. (Oxford: Oxford University Press, 1933), p. 307ff.
4. Andrew Cornes, *Divorce and Remarriage* (London: Hodder and Stoughton, 1994), pp. 131–79.
5. Atkinson, *Pastoral Ethics*, (Oxford: Lynx Communications, 1994), p. 29.
6. A. E. Harvey, *Promise or Pretence?* (London: SCM Press, 1994), p. 16.
7. If the situation that lies behind Ezra's solution to the problem of mixed marriages – viz. enforced divorce – is similar to what lies behind Malachi's strictures, then some of the seeming injustice is taken out of Ezra's action. It is not a question (in our terms) of innocent romance – or arrangements – between free agents, but harsh pandering to male power. Ezra's action would then be at least part way towards restoring the *status quo ante* and the possible reinstatement of Jewish wives. But if the situation was like this, he does not say so, thus no argument may hang on this point.
8. A tradition of interpreting Genesis 1 and 2 as a prohibition of second marriage (either by polygamy or after divorce) also surfaces clearly at Qumran in the Damascus Document of c. 100 BCE. (G. Vermes, *The Dead Sea Scrolls in English* (London: Penguin, 1962), p. 101). The argument there seems to be that God created, and then at the flood redeemed,

humankind in pairs, thus favouring monogamous marriage. Malachi seems to be linking the oneness of God and the unity between man and wife in the creation ordinance of marriage.
9. A modern application of this idea need not, of course, be limited to military service or the husband working away from home. Other pressures on a new family might be the threat of repossession of a mortgaged house, for instance.

FOUR

New Testament – Marriage and Divorce

The gospels

Discussion of marriage and divorce occurs in several places in the New Testament. The gospels cite individual sayings of our Lord about divorce and a longer argument with the Pharisees about it. In the 'household codes' in some of the letters of Paul and others the duties of spouses are touched upon, and in 1 Corinthians Paul writes at some length about separation. In both contexts singleness is spoken about with favour. The setting of all the teaching about marriage (and divorce) is one in which other features of the Christian lifestyle are discussed – it is not a subject to be isolated from Christian behaviour and the Christian attitude to morality in general.

We also read of incidents and encounters in our Lord's ministry which illuminate the way he dealt with people. This pastoral practice sometimes seems at variance with the strict letter of his ethical instructions. It is tempting to speculate how far Jesus' own family background and especially Joseph's experience (Matthew 1:19f.) influenced his thinking!

Incidents and encounters

Two incidents from our Lord's ministry relate to divorce, though neither actually mention it. The first is his encounter with the Samaritan woman at the well near Sychar (John 4:4–30) and the other is that of the woman caught in the act of adultery (John 8:1–11). Both show his relaxed attitude of respect towards women, whom he appears to have listened to as people in their own right and as equals. St John tells us that this attitude surprised his followers, at least at that early stage in his career (John 4:27), though Luke implies that it was a natural part of his ministry (Luke 8:2–3). Some, at least, of Jesus' rabbinical contemporaries had raised their paranoia in the presence of women to an art form in ways which surely coloured their attitudes to married life and divorce.[1] Thus when St Peter (1 Peter 3:7) speaks of wives as joint heirs with their husbands of the grace of life, he is not stating the obvious, but repeating a lesson he learned from his master and challenging conventional male wisdom. Obvious though it may seem in the twentieth-century, Jesus' respect for the equality of women in a very unequal society is the key mark of his teaching on marriage and divorce. (In fact, it may not be so obvious in the twentieth-century; how much will the sparring between the sexes, and the superior and domineering attitude of the lads whom I observe in an open youth club be sowing seeds for later unstable, unequal or disloyal marriages?)

I have suggested elsewhere that Jesus' aim in asking to meet the Samaritan's husband was not to expose her sinful past, but to straighten out her troubled present.[2] It may also have been a thoughtful and kind gesture towards her, since if her current man had heard that she had been seen in public talking to another man, he might treat that as something unseemly in his eyes and get rid of her, even though they were not formally married. She was probably middle-aged (unless her previous marriages had been very brief) and in a very vulnerable situation, with no source of dowry from her family which might attract a committed husband and insure her against casual divorce. We misrepresent her, I believe, if we see her as the gay divorcee or even the merry widow. She was approaching what was, by the standards of the day, old age and had become dependent on whoever would take her on – perhaps more as a drawer of water than as a 'common law' wife. Multiple bereavement or divorce had driven her towards an irregular liaison. As Jesus was to express it later when preaching the Sermon on the Mount, 'When a man divorces his wife ... he makes her commit adultery' (Matthew 5:32).

St John does not actually state that she had ever been divorced, though it is not denied either. In any case, under the law then prevailing, a divorce could not be at her instigation (unless a court recognized her claim that her husband had contracted a disease such as leprosy or had undertaken unclean work such as tanning and required, on her behalf, that he divorce her. She could, of course, have provoked it by her actions. It is also possible that as a Samaritan she had the ability not to consent to divorce, though the evidence for that is not clear.[3] The most that can be said from the actual text (and that is by reading a great deal into the nuances of the order of the Greek words) is that the man in question was not *her* husband but possibly someone else's. In that case, it was the man's relationship with women that Jesus wanted to straighten out (for her benefit, I suggest) as much as her own past. It could of course have been that she had enticed the man away from his proper wife, which might explain why she had to collect water at the hot and anti-social hour of midday, but her subsequent openness to the (supposedly) censorious crowd about someone who 'told me all that I ever did' suggests that that was not the case.

Whether divorce is part of this story or not, what we see here is Jesus working towards a better future for a person whom circumstances or sin have left socially weak and emotionally vulnerable. For her 'salvation' meant not only meeting and trusting the Messiah, but seeing her family life set by him on firm foundations. What those foundations were is not clear from the story as told. However, Jesus' approach was pastoral rather than legalistic when he was dealing with the needs of an individual whom he met. This approach looked forward rather than back.

The same may be said of the other incident involving the woman caught in the act of adultery. Here was a story that so captured Christian imagination as a portrait of Jesus' forgiving love that it could not be forgotten and was included in the gospel narrative in a way that no other free-floating story was. A married woman is hauled before Jesus having been caught with another man (where was he?), betraying her husband. Jewish practice at the time appears to have required the husband in such cases to divorce the wife. Mosaic law actually prescribed stoning for such a crime, though standards of proof in Jewish courts, their deep humanity, and their loss of independent authority to use the death penalty meant that the Mosaic penalty was not exacted. The Pharisees no doubt knew that Jesus had claimed to come to fulfil the Law. If Matthew accurately records his teaching, Jesus recognized that a cuckolded husband had the right to divorce his wife (Matthew 5:32), though he speaks as if he did not require such action of his followers. The Pharisees put him on the spot: Would he renege on the Law? Would he defy Rome and sanction a death sentence? Would he condone a woman's offence against her husband? In many ways his response is puzzling and we are teased by what we are not told. What is clear, however, is that he forced powerful men to realize that they were just as much sinners as a weakly-placed woman. He did not pronounce a legal judgement against her, but he did not condone her action either. She was to carry on her life and from then on not sin again. What she had done was wrong, Jesus states gently, but what was important was what happened from then on. Once again, Jesus' practice was pastoral in a face-to-face situation. He looked to getting the future right rather than enforcing a law and he defended those whom society picked on in the way it used its laws. This is what we should expect if St John is right in characterizing Jesus' whole life in the words: 'The Law was given through Moses; generosity and integrity came into being through Jesus Christ.' (1:17).

A further incident, which supports my view that Jesus' pastoral practice was far from legalistic, and shows his understanding of people's motives and sympathy with outsiders whose relationships were irregular or in a mess, is that of his treatment of the lady of the city, in Luke 7:36ff., at the supper party with Simon the Pharisee; whatever his general teaching or some earlier conversation with her had led her to do by way of repentance and reformation, his pastoral care of her demonstrated support and defence when those with influence wanted to exclude her. He had listened to her story or observed her closely enough to know her motives and feelings, and to understand (v. 47).

Jesus' teaching
One of the underlying motives in Jesus' pastoral practice was a concern for those who were oppressed – for example, women

who, given the way society organized itself, were vulnerable to male abuse. Jesus did not use the language of political theory to express this concern; the language he was familiar with was personal, not theoretical. It was 'mighty people' who were to be 'dethroned' and God's 'humble poor lifted high'; the hungry would be fed and the rich sent away empty, according to the hymn which surely best expresses thinking in the milieu in which he grew up (Mary's song of praise: Luke 1:46ff.). His own manifesto, citing verses from Isaiah, expresses the same (Luke 4:16–21), as does a typical sermon (Luke 6:27–31). Similarly, his teaching which relates specifically to marriage is expressed in direct and personal terms, using the vocabulary available to him to make a point and change behaviour and attitudes, not to engage in an abstract discussion. Thus in his teaching we find mental stripping classed as adultery (Matthew 5:27ff.), as is divorce, though his contemporaries legislated for it quite happily. In Matthew 5:32, Jesus goes further. He says that a woman is pushed into a situation as bad as adultery when she is divorced. In saying that, he is siding with the woman in the case. His contemporaries saw adultery only as an offence against the husband, not the woman.

In the Sermon on the Mount (from which these two verses come) we find Jesus talking about the lifestyle he expected within the kingdom of God. Peacemaking and purity, mercy and meekness (a strong humility) characterize the children of the kingdom. The Law in all its fullness is to be fulfilled. Insults and destructive words are to be avoided as next to murder; generosity replaces vengeance, and love transforms hate. These virtues apply to those within the kingdom in all their relationships, and therefore should be seen in marriages within the kingdom too. Jesus said very little about how married couples should get on because he had already said what was needed for a wider set of circumstances.

This sermon also sets priorities for the people of God. In very graphic terms Jesus tells his followers that personal comfort and convenience are not absolute rights or eternal values. If your right eye trips you up, throw it away! (5:29) It is better to enter life maimed than to go comfortably to hell. (This was taught specifically in the context of sexual matters.) Similarly, the right way to deal with unfair demands may be to go the extra mile rather than to go on an assertiveness training course (5:39ff.). The logic behind this is that it reflects the generous character of God himself. Also, to draw in what Jesus says in Matthew 18:15ff. about conciliation within the kingdom community, it forms a basis for talking through the unfairness and the tensions which can arise, for example, within a step-family, and may shame the offender into repentance (as Paul suggests in Romans 12:14–21, which may be a conscious application of this part of Jesus' teaching).

Jesus on divorce

So what did Jesus say about divorce? Jesus' approach was in contrast with the rabbis', whose concern was with correct procedures and the validity of bills of divorce. At least that seems (to a modern observer) the case by the time the *Mishnah* was compiled a century and more later.[4] Perhaps the way Jesus cites their deduction from Deuteronomy 24 in Matthew 5:31 highlights their focus of attention in his day also. What they thought of in terms of routine legal procedure, Jesus, in the graphic directness we have already seen, categorizes as incitement to adultery: 'I tell you, everyone who dismisses his wife (apart from grounds of immorality) makes her suffer adultery, and whoever marries a divorced woman commits adultery' (Matthew 5:32).

This is a difficult text and some manuscripts actually leave out the final clause. Perhaps it was difficult for Matthew and those who copied his text to grasp the implications of what Jesus was saying, for the Hebrew word for 'adultery' would not normally be used in connection with a woman who was not, or was no longer, married. Adultery offended the husband's rights and honour: it adulterated her for him. Jesus, however, is looking at the situation from the wife's point of view. If she has not been immoral, at the very least she is being painted as such. (This is one interpretation of the difficult phrase that I have rendered 'makes her suffer adultery', i.e. 'makes her out to be an adulteress'.) More likely he means that she is forced to look for a new husband, since dowries were difficult to recover and there was no support outside a family for a woman alone. Her rights and honour are infringed, and she is likely to have to act immorally to find maintenance, even though the traditional laws specified a one-off payment for maintenance at the time of the divorce if she had not committed some alleged marital offence.[5]

A similar saying is in Luke 16:18. At first this chapter appears to be an almost random collection of sayings and parables, but a common thread is discernable. Jesus is speaking here in support of the poor and socially weak. That Luke has collected such teaching together indicates how he saw the position of a divorced woman. 'Everyone who dismisses his wife and marries another is committing adultery, and the man who marries someone divorced from her husband is committing adultery.' In this verse the emphasis seems to be on remarriage as the act that is adulterous. In the first clause the offended party is the first wife; in the second, the offended party is the first husband, which would be more in accord with conventional wisdom at the time (except that he had ostensibly surrendered his interest in her). The same could be said of the final clause in Matthew's version of this saying.

The implication seen in this clause (since the days of the early Church) has been that somehow the marriage has not ended morally and spiritually, even if the Law says otherwise – at least for a marriage within God's people. I find it difficult to believe, however, that Jesus was saying that there is still some *metaphysical* bond in existence, largely because metaphysics was not a Hebrew way of thinking. But he says many things about marriage that are out of keeping with his contemporaries' thinking and such a novel approach may be possible. More likely he is saying that *moral* bonds still exist and that the couple still have responsibilities to each other. The close personal obligations of marriage – and its economic implications connected with dowries and maintenance – cannot just be shrugged aside. It would be tempting to add that the emotional bonds are still there, even if the divorcing party denies it. This, however, would be anachronistic, for it is the twentieth century that has 'discovered' emotions. But Jesus' understanding of human feelings and behaviour was out of his time, so such an interpretation might also be possible.

What was Jesus' motive in saying this? Was he acting as a legislator, saying to his followers, 'Thou shalt not divorce'? Or was he using a parabolic way of teaching in order to bring out the enormity of divorce? 'If you divorce and remarry you are as good as breaking one of the Ten Commandments, so don't think about it! Divorce is not just a simple legal procedure to get right. It is a sin because of what it does to the other people involved.' I am inclined to accept the latter in which Jesus gives his followers the moral choice to respond if they have ears to hear.[6] Elsewhere in the Sermon on the Mount Matthew records Jesus teaching by means of a parable that sounds like a command (5:25f.). 'Make peace with your accuser . . .' is not simply thrown in, almost at random, as a piece of sound advice for those involved in litigation, but is saying parabolically: 'You know how seriously you would act on a secular level to sort out a dispute; how much more serious is a dispute, however minor it seems, which has eternal consequences!'

Testing questions

The fullest teaching on divorce and marriage comes in Matthew 19 and Mark 10. Both passages are set across the Jordan from Judaea proper, in partly Gentile country near Herod's winter palace at Jericho. The location is significant, partly because of the recent marriage of Herod Antipas to his brother Philip's wife. She had divorced Philip using Roman legal processes – an event which had led indirectly to the death of John the Baptist, Jesus' cousin (cf. Mark 6:7ff.). Also, in an area of mixed population, the Jewish Law, which did not allow for a wife's initiative in divorcing her husband, might be less dominant. Among Jews in Egypt the Law was not strictly adhered to,[7] while even in the *Mishnah* a woman may be involved in writing the divorce papers. Thus the argument that Mark 10:12 (which speaks of a woman divorcing her husband) was added by the gospel writer for a Roman audience need not hold water.

The two texts read as follows:

Matthew 19

3. Some Pharisees approached him and put him on the spot by saying, 'Is it lawful for someone to divorce his wife for every reason?'

4. In reply he said, 'Did you not read that from the beginning the Creator made them male and female?'
5. and he said, 'for this reason a person will leave his father and mother and will be attached to his wife, and the two will become one flesh"?
6. Therefore they are no longer two, but one flesh. What, therefore, God has yoked together, a person is not to separate.'
7. They said to him, 'So why did Moses instruct the giving of a bill of dismissal and divorce?'
8. He said to them, 'Moses, because of your hard-heartedness, permitted you to divorce your wives, but from the beginning it was not so.

9. But I say to you that whoever divorces his wife on grounds other than immorality and marries another is committing adultery.'

Mark 10

2. Approaching him some Pharisees asked whether it is lawful for a husband to divorce a wife. They were putting him on the spot.
3. In reply he said to them, 'What did Moses instruct you?'
4. They said, 'Moses permitted the writing of a bill of dismissal, and divorce.'
5. But Jesus said to them, 'it was because of your hard-heartedness that he wrote for you this instruction.
6. But from the beginning of creation He "made them male and female".
7. "For this reason a person will leave his/her father and his/her mother,
8. and the two will become one flesh."
9. Therefore they are no longer two but one flesh. What, therefore, God has yoked together, a person is not to separate.'

10. Indoors the disciples asked him about this again,
11. and he said to them, 'Whoever divorces his wife and marries another is committing adultery against her.
12. And if she herself after divorcing her husband marries another, she is committing adultery.'

Matthew continues with some unique teaching on marriage and singleness, which illustrates how radical the disciples found what Jesus had said:

> 10. The disciples said to him, 'If that is the case for a person with his wife, it is not a good thing to marry!'
> 11. He said to them, 'Not everyone can take this saying, but it is for those to whom it is given.
> 12. There are, you see, some eunuchs who were born that way from their mother's womb; and there are some eunuchs who were made eunuchs by people; and there are some eunuchs who made themselves eunuchs for the sake of the kingdom of heaven. If someone is able to take this, let him do so.'

Matthew 19 follows Matthew 18 in the teaching structure of Matthew's gospel, though he recognizes a lapse of time between the two in his historical framework. That is not a banal truism; Matthew 18 is a sermon on human value before God, in which the child is the greatest; of human moral priorities in the face of temptation and hardship (cf. 5:30 before v. 32); and of Christian forgiveness and attempts at reconciliation in the face of sin, attempts which he recognized might not succeed (v. 17). Faced by such lack of success Jesus recognized that a grievous separation might be the only answer. As elsewhere, we are intended by the gospel writer to hear teaching about marriage in the context of wider moral instruction which offers a pattern for Marriage Guidance Counselling and conciliation.

The way the Pharisees were trying to trick Jesus may have been connected with the Herods' affairs. Would he say something, perhaps provoked by his cousin's recent execution, that could put his head on the block too? The way Matthew reports the question, however, sets it in the context of the debate between Shammai and Hillel referred to above. Hillel's followers argued that divorce was permissible for a wide range of reasons; Shammaites might well exaggerate this into 'any kind of reason'. The trick could simply have been to get him to take sides in this dispute. There may also be a contrast between the words 'instruct' and 'permit', though in some contexts the Greek word for 'permit' used here can mean 'instruct'! If there is a contrast intended, then in Mark Jesus is asking what the Law commands and the Pharisees quote the permissive legislation on which they based all their arguments. Jesus regards this as secondary to the creation ordinance. In Matthew, where the contrast is clearer, Jesus points out that Moses did not *command* divorce, but *permitted* it as a concession to human stubbornness.

Jesus then reminds them of God's original plan. We have already noted how Malachi appears to have looked back to Genesis 2 in his plea for lifelong loyalty in marriage, and how the sectaries of Qumran (just over the horizon from where Jesus was talking) used these verses certainly to argue against polygamy (for they quoted the 'two by two' detail of the story of the Ark) and, by implication, against remarriage too. In using the pattern set out in Genesis 2 as definitive, Jesus is not simply capping one text with another. He is appealing to the best information he had as to the way God made the world and the human race. He is inviting his hearers to let their moral practice and attitudes be shaped by the way God acts, just as he had invited them to consider God's lilies in the field or his rain falling on the just and unjust, in order to shape their attitude to wealth or vengeance.

Genesis 2:24 combines description and teaching and notes the way God brings together the archetypal man and woman as husband and wife as normative for all marital relationships. The ties of birth – loyalty to one's own flesh and blood – become less binding than the sexual and emotional ties of marriage (though no rite of marriage is laid down other than leaving and cleaving, independent action and commitment, which create a moral bond of their own). There is delight and romance (an anachronistic word, I know, but even the wise men of the Old Testament knew the mystery of romantic attraction – cf. Proverbs 30:18f.) and there is openness and frank sharing of body and personality – they were naked and not ashamed, fit helpers to support each other in life's richness or poverty. All these things are there in the description of the creation ordinance of marriage, and to it Jesus appeals. One-to-one commitment and the rewards that stem from it are what God intended in creation, and it is to be lived out in the new creation that the Messiah brings. What God joined in the Genesis narrative, and the way he joined it should be the governing principle both in interpreting the Law for the age that is now (Jesus tells the Pharisees), and for living in the age to come which (Jesus taught) begins from now for those 'to whom it is given'.

Neither Genesis nor Jesus are saying that God 'gives away' *every* bride in so specific a way as he selected Eve for Adam, or that every single marriage is 'joined, yoked together' by God. (Every couple, however, may ask 'Are we two together called to this holy estate?') Still less are they implying that a couple may be joined together by God in some mystical union, even if they themselves missed the opportunity through shyness or wilfulness! (The idea of such 'spiritual unions' owes much to the nineteenth-century spiritualists, some of whom were looking to justify illicit affairs.) Yet each couple reflects the eternal standard more or less closely in the bonds they have entered into by whatever process their culture guides them. They are called – for their own benefit and that of all other couples, and out of reverence for their creator – not to undermine that standard in the way they may try to put each other asunder. Jesus is not implying that somehow every individual marriage is 'there', an eternal verity in heaven. Perhaps he is suggesting that the moral ideal of marriage – one-to-one commitment of a man and woman for life, to the exclusion of any other – is an eternal verity as well as an earthly pattern, deriving from the very roots of creation, which we diminish and threaten if we put our own relationships asunder. (In trying to understand him in this way, however, I am conscious of using an Idealist way of speaking which is more at home in the Greek thought of that time than the Jewish.)

In translating Matthew 19 and Mark 10 I have been careful to distinguish between the Greek words for 'man' (i.e. a male human being) and 'husband' on the one hand, and 'person' (i.e. a human being of either sex) on the other, even where this makes for clumsy English. His/her in Mark 10:7 is in fact simply 'the' in the Greek, but contrasts with Matthew who leaves out any article or possessive pronoun. I have also kept the phrase 'one flesh'. The Hebrew words behind this imply more than the physical nature, but a moral and personal unity, as in Isaiah's phrase, 'All flesh is grass', meaning all humanity. This moral unity, however, would not have implied in Jesus' day the legal unity that English lawyers and legislators in the nineteenth century tried to import into it as the basis for a wife and husband being treated as one 'person' in law.

The sentence 'What God has yoked, a person is not to separate' was not directed primarily at divorce courts, for there were none, but at individual people who might provoke a divorce by hard-heartedness or seduction, and at rabbis who argued for its ease.

In neither Matthew nor Mark does Jesus actually say that Moses was wrong to permit divorce. If his teaching (as recorded in Matthew 5) was well known, the Pharisees' trick may have been to try to get him to set aside something in the Law because of his strong views against divorce. What Jesus does say is that divorce was second-best, allowed because of human recalcitrance, not God's original intention. That this might continue to be the case, even after the coming of the kingdom, seems to have been in Jesus' mind too if the recognition that 'not everyone can take this saying' applies not to the disciples' words 'it is not a good thing to marry', but to his earlier equation of divorce and adultery. The question then remains: who are those 'to whom it is given'? The eunuchs to whom Jesus refers may be literally, emotionally or metaphorically deprived. The paragraph again shows Jesus' understanding and sympathy for people who have been ill-treated by those with power, and the high value he placed on self-sacrifice for his cause. Thus as we discuss marriage and family values we should not underrate singleness and celibacy.

Though Matthew and Mark appear to be describing the same incident, there are differences in their accounts which come to a head with the final saying about divorce and remarriage. The explanation most often offered nowadays is that each gospel writer retold the event in terms appropriate to his audience. If Mark wrote first – possibly in Rome amid a society which took divorce very lightly – then he retains Jesus' striking insistence on lifelong commitment in marriage. He also includes Jesus' defence of a woman's rights when he said that her husband could commit adultery 'against her'. (Or perhaps Mark added these words to bring out clearly the implication of what Jesus said?) Mark then adds a specific application to Roman society, where women could initiate divorce proceedings. However, as we noted earlier, the setting of this paragraph in the life of Jesus offers just as convincing an explanation of why Jesus might speak of a woman divorcing her husband. He already knew (cf. Luke 13:31f.) that he had no reason to back away from a challenge to the Herods' morals. Matthew then, taking Mark as his basis, meets the needs and questions of a largely Jewish church in western Syria brought up on the Hillel/Shammai debate by recasting the story in terms of that debate. He leaves out the verse about a woman initiating divorce since its relevance was largely Roman – or was simply a historical reference – and adds what his readers would expect – permission (as per Shammai) to divorce a wife on grounds of her immoral conduct – or perhaps he is simply making clear what he believed Jesus implied.

This excursion into the theories of gospel composition is not merely an academic exercise. If the 'Matthean exception' is held by biblical scholars to come literally from Matthew (who may not indeed have been Matthew the apostle anyway) and not Jesus, it affects the moralists' arguments. This is in fact what happened in the early nineteen hundreds when churchmen who wished to resist the extension of divorce law found their case strengthened. Those who had been willing to accept divorce on the grounds found in scripture – adultery or desertion – had to search around for other arguments, such as the suggestion that Jesus had never intended his words to be applied as legislation but as moral encouragement.[8]

There are two false premises in this argument: firstly, that Jesus only ever talked about a subject once; and secondly, that the relationship between near-parallel texts such as those above is purely literary – one author cribbing off the other, and then making his own changes for theological motives. Even cloistered academics sometimes use the same lecture notes twice or adapt a precise turn of phrase to suit their listeners' interests. As an itinerant pastor and teacher Jesus must have faced the same questions and given the same messages on many different occasions, with different audiences but at times the same old hecklers! There was one memorable occasion opposite Jericho when Jesus was heckled over his attitude to divorce, and around that incident the two writers (one using the other as his main source) have gathered what they remember or have learned of Jesus' teaching on the subject. The memories of each are perhaps prompted by what he has found relevant for his churches.

So did Jesus allow divorce on the grounds of (the wife's) adultery, as Matthew twice reports but none of the other gospel writers mention? Mark makes no mention of such an exception. However as he reports the incident, there is no need for one. His point is to emphasize that divorce is not a creation ordinance and not part of God's best intentions for humankind. His intention is to remind an audience for whom divorce was perhaps a source of prurient gossip that Jesus told them not even to contemplate it. To mention an exception would be to weaken the point. Matthew's audience approached divorce differently. For them it had been a subject of theological debate, and they knew that there was an exception implied in the Law. Where did Jesus stand in that debate? Matthew's memory, perhaps sharpened by many discussions of the point, focuses on how Jesus handled the debate. Thus his verse 9 answers the question his report began with. Jesus is saying, 'Actually both Hillel and Shammai got it wrong. Divorce was never God's primary intention. But when it comes to the crunch, Shammai was nearer the mark, though Moses did not *command* divorce even in the circumstances of adultery.' Therefore, Jesus did allow the exception in the discussion Matthew reports here, and also in the single saying recorded in Matthew 5:32. St Paul supports this view when he is ready to allow another exception (1 Corinthians 7:15), suggesting that he knew that Christ had already permitted one.

That, however, is not to suggest that Jesus lightly accepted that people would divorce. The casual disposal of another human being to whom one has been intimately related is not to be contemplated, and neither is the deliberate sundering of a relationship that fulfils God's plans in creation. The easy adoption of a person so cast off is in fact connivance with the first husband's sin and also tantamount to adultery. Where the wife is in a position to take action to dispose of her husband – through the use of a non-Jewish legal process or by her provocation, or by choosing to take exception to his job or his health – she comes under the same criticism.

The one party whom Jesus does not criticize in any of the texts is the divorced but otherwise chaste wife. It is with some sympathy that he recognizes that she is being forced into adultery in order to maintain herself (Matthew 5:32). This was not the kind of treatment for which God created people! Jesus' motive in denouncing divorce was the protection of the weak in a system in which divorce had become (at least in the hands of Hillel's followers and Gentile cultures) a means of abuse and ill-treatment. If that was the spirit behind the letter of what he said, we too should be acting on that motive and asking how we may go and do likewise. Might reluctant acceptance of divorce, with the likelihood of remarriage as the most feasible means of human support, be the least bad course of action when a marriage has become a means of abuse and reconciliation fails? St Paul seems to have thought and taught so.

The epistles

I have suggested that points about marriage made in other parts of the New Testament are applications of Jesus' teaching, and that wider teaching about the Christian life is assumed when advice about married life is given. The most significant passages in the New Testament epistles are Ephesians 4–6 – especially parts of chapter 5 – and its parallel in Colossians 3; 1 Corinthians 7; 1 Peter 3; and some verses of 1 Timothy 3 and 5. Elsewhere there are isolated verses which warn against sexual laxity and urge that 'the marriage bed be undefiled' (e.g. Hebrews 13:4). The translation in 1 Thessalonians 4:4 is uncertain and probably refers to sexual self-control. Marriage is also used as a parable in Romans 7.

Ephesians – marriage reflecting God's love

Paul's alleged teaching in Ephesians has earned him a bad reputation as a misogynist. I say 'alleged' because he has been quoted selectively, initially by men wishing to support their own positions of power in the family and society, and latterly by those who criticize that position. True, he does say, 'Wives, obey your husbands', and that phrase is featured in the *Book of Common Prayer* marriage service, so that brides-to-be still ask whether they have to promise to obey. But if we look more closely at that phrase, we see that simple acceptance misrepresents Paul and almost reverses his teaching.

The verse in question (Ephesians 5:22) follows one which tells all Christian people to be subject to one another, and is in fact grammatically dependent on it since it otherwise lacks a verb. It is followed by an even more striking verse (25), which challenges husbands to love their wives with the same sacrificial love that is seen in Christ himself and his self-offering on behalf of his Church. If we limit ourselves for the moment to chapter 5, Paul has called all the Christians at Ephesus – husbands, wives, singles, widows and widowers – to live loving lives, imitating God in Christ and reflecting his self-sacrifice. He then points out that immoral sexual behaviour, or gossip and titivating discussion about it, has no place among Christians any more than a range of other sins which he treats on a par with sexual sin. Economic greed is as deadly as adultery. They should support each other in a life shaped by God-centred gratitude. Within that context they should rank others' wishes higher than their own.

When the men in Ephesus heard Paul specifically apply that message to the way wives were to rank their own husbands more highly than themselves, I can see them leaning forward on their benches nodding vigorously. 'That's right, Paul,' one can almost hear them saying, 'you tell them!' After all, that is what they would expect whether their background was Jewish or Gentile. A respectable woman was very much under her husband's direction and kept a low profile in public, even if she played a responsible part in running the household and any servants it contained. However Paul elaborates. The husband has a Christ-like role within the marriage, he says, drawing on the ancient parable in the teachings of Hosea, Isaiah and Jeremiah in which God was husband to Israel's wife. The he hits them: 'OK, husbands, if you have a Christ-like role in marriage, listen to what it means. Christ gave himself up for the Church, his death (remembered in the waters of baptism) prepared his bride [who might, in the marriage rites of the day, prepare for her wedding with a bath that was symbolic as well as practical]. His example should mould your relationship, husbands, to your wives.' This idea was ahead of its time. Paul could not rely on his rhetorical trick, or the moral example of Christ himself, to transform the men's thinking so that it did not conform to that of the world around them. He argues his case in words which, to twentieth-century ears, sound condescending, but which were aimed at demonstrating the practicality of his case: You take care of your own body. Your wife is as good as your own self; love her as yourself.

It may seem special pleading, a wisdom by hindsight, which sees Paul as a cryptofeminist. The idea is too far out of its time to be true! But on the contrary, Paul fills this letter with ideas out of their time, such as a breaking down of the barriers between Jew and Gentile, and slave-owners treating their slaves with forbearance and humility. And Paul goes on to make similar points in other letters. In Galatians he goes as far as saying that there is no distinction between Jew and Gentile, slave or free, male or female. In 1 Thessalonians 4 he specifically tells his readers not to let their conduct in connection with marriage be shaped by the pagan practice of the time. In 1 Corinthians 7 he speaks of a wife being master of her husband's body. What should be more natural within the Christian Church than that a husband should want the best for his wife if they have taken to heart the general teaching in Ephesians 4? That teaches that we should speak the truth in love – or better, 'live out the Gospel message with loving integrity' – and seek to grow into Christ-like maturity, not letting the sun go down on anger, conversing positively and wholesomely, being kind and forgiving in imitation of God, who in Christ forgives both husband and wife.

Paul goes on to speak of the union of husband and wife as representing a great mystery. This is perhaps an aside to Paul's main argument. Husbands should love their wives as their own bodies because of the moral and emotional union which makes them one flesh, as God intended (5:31). The practical application of this is love and respect (5:33). But in Ephesians Paul has a great deal to say about God's hidden plan now revealed to the apostles and prophets – God's great mystery made plain, in which the benefits of a relationship with him are made available in union with Christ to Gentile as well as Jew, for all the world and its powers to see (3:10f.). That mystery dates from God's purpose in creation (3:9, cf. Romans 1:19–20). So in quoting words spoken in the beginning about marriage, Paul notes how they hold a deeper meaning which corresponds to his major theme in the letter. Where we see a husband and wife caring and supporting each other in loving marriage, there we see a reflection of God's love and a sign of his care for his people.

To sum up, Paul's intention is to change his hearers' (especially his male hearers') moral views and their consequent treatment of their spouses. He has a high view of marriage as a relationship which can reflect the love of Christ for his Church. But he is giving moral advice in which he uses the imitation of Christ as a motive for Christian action, rather than a metaphysic of marriage. In writing this way he was perhaps conscious of Jesus' own high regard for the women he met.

1 Corinthians – a 'Pauline privilege'?

In his letters to the church at Corinth Paul deals with practical moral questions that came up in their common life and responds either to direct questions or reports of their conduct which visitors brought him. The Corinthians carried over a number of pagan ideas into their Christian practice. They also misunderstood the liberty Christ gave them as a licence for immoral behaviour. In 1 Corinthians 5 Paul has on the one hand to warn against resorting to prostitutes, and on the other to condemn a form of incest. In chapter 6 he describes conduct which is unworthy of the kingdom of God – conduct which includes, but is not restricted to, sexual immorality. Thus, when thinking about sexual sins and the problem of divorce we should not exaggerate them as *the* sins which are more heinous than any other, though Paul does suggest that their very personal and intimate nature threatens the person (*soma* – body) of the sinner in a particularly gripping way.

Paul then turns to deal with a question that was to bedevil Christian thinking about sexuality and marriage for centuries. It was a very live and real one in his cultural environment and it derived from the deep suspicion that many Greeks felt towards the physical body. This slogan by one of their philosophers sums up the mood: *soma sema*, roughly 'the womb's a tomb'. If the highest form of being was the intellectual and spiritual, then the material world was an accident and an aberration. Passion, in which the intellectual self lost control and was governed by the forces of the body or of lower nature, was to be rejected. It was a form of suffering which the truly wise man avoided. That avoidance could take different forms, and Paul had to expose the evil in both of them. At one extreme came asceticism: 'It is well for a man not to touch a woman' (7:1, cf. 1 Timothy 4:3). At the other, it could lead to a detached hedonism which gave in to all forms of passion but claimed to remain intellectually aloof from what the body went through. There may be signs of such errors in the letters to Colossae and Ephesus, but it was later Christians who had to argue most strongly against this development. Paul knows all too well the power of sinful passions, but is sure that the physical body is 'for the Lord' and that the Corinthians are personally (bodily) temples of the Holy Spirit within them (6:13, 19). The married life, with its sexual aspect, is therefore a sphere in which God is at work and in which he can be glorified.

Paul's methods and motives are informative here. To combat the asceticism which suggested that sexual intercourse was somehow tainted and sinful even within marriage, he affirms that husband and wife should give each other their marital rights. In saying this he is perhaps following a rabbinic tradition in which advice was given on how frequently men of different trades should have intercourse with their wives. This duty was held to be stronger than a vow. He is less prescriptive in this, however, than the rabbis (at least as they were reported a hundred or so years later). Paul offers some advice on the basis of personal experience while recognizing that all individuals have their own particular gift from God. What is perhaps distinctive is that he delineates the wife's rights as clearly and as equally as her husband's. The husband belongs to the wife in person, not to himself (7:4).

In 7:8ff. he again refers to his own circumstances in advising the unmarried and widowed to remain single – though he recognizes the preferability of marriage to the pain of unfulfilled sexual drives. He was a realist, aware of the power of the instincts or 'passions' as he would probably have termed them.

Then, in advising the married members of the church, he specifically refers to the Lord's teaching that husband and wife should not separate, which he quotes in different words from the gospel writers. In quoting it, however, he immediately recognizes that it may be broken: in 7:11 he adds parenthetically 'but if she does separate . . .' This, of course, could be part of the quotation. Either way, the possibility is recognized that the Lord's ideals may not be met, yet those ideals are affirmed. Separation between Christian spouses should not take place, and if it does, they should not go looking for another partner but should seek reconciliation.

Having quoted the Lord where he knows his specific teaching, Paul then offers his own advice for circumstances which Jesus did not meet among his audience in a predominantly Jewish community. In Jesus' situation, mixed marriages would have been rare and a social dichotomy had not yet arisen between his followers and other communities. The fact that Paul felt free, conscientiously seeking the Spirit's guidance (7:40), to extend and adapt Jesus' teaching and add an additional reason why divorce might be possible, is as significant as what he actually says. He recognizes that in a mixed marriage, where one partner has become a Christian and the other not, there may be difficulties and the unbelieving partner may wish to go his own way (7:12–15). While the Church was a distinct group within a largely pagan world this was to be an ongoing problem to which later Christian writers such as Tertullian refer. When her husband expects wifely duty and home-centred pursuits, a wife's wish to visit the sick or poor in their homes or to attend a night-time vigil at another home will cause friction. In such circumstances the believing partner should not take the initiative in separating. The motive Paul offers for this is different from that put forward when both are Christians. Here evangelistic opportunity weighs heavily in his thinking. Peter says something similar in 1 Peter 3:1, suggesting that this was a common way of thinking and evangelizing in the early Church. By sticking with the difficult marriage the believing wife may win her husband over. In any case, her presence sanctifies the household (7:14).

If, however, the unbeliever goes his or her own way, then the believing partner is 'not enslaved' (7:15). Does he mean that they are free to divorce, or that, having been divorced, they are not bound to a relationship that has ceased when a partner has gone? I take it to be the latter, if only because the divorce has already been effected by the other partner: the believer does not need to seek 'emancipation' because it has already been imposed. Though in some cases a couple (or their families) might argue over repayment of a dowry or compensation, there were no courts in which a divorce might be contested. Where the marriage had begun in the more informal ways open to non-citizens in the Roman Empire, divorce was itself a very informal affair. In which case, what Paul is saying is that believers are then free to remarry.

There is, however, a complication, caused, as so often, by a very tiny word. In Greek it was normal for every sentence to be connected with the previous one by a conjunction which indicates the logical development of the thought. Paul continues: 'In peace God has called us.' Here we might expect the connecting word to be 'for'. In fact it is a gentle 'but', in spite of what the RSV says. He is not saying, 'Separate (and remarry) for God wants you to be at peace', but 'Separate (and remarry) if you have no other choice, but the overriding intention should be the peace of God drawn into the way the first marriage develops.' (cf. Barratt in loc.)[9]

Paul was aware of the 'Matthean exception' and perhaps alludes to it in 7:11. This no doubt gave him the confidence to advise on other possible exceptions to the ideal. He was asking the practical questions: Would witness within the marriage save the unbelieving partner? If not, was the marriage working or had it failed? This is, therefore, a new exception. However, is it legitimate to apply it only in terms of believers and unbelievers, or can it be extended in its turn to any marriage which is not working? One way in which it should not be applied is as a means of wriggling out of a marriage. Paul did not intend it as a ploy by which ecclesiastical lawyers could justify an annulment on grounds of disparity of beliefs.

One way in which the peace of God may be found is in acceptance of the situation in which a person is called to be a Christian. Paul offers some illustrations of how this will work in other aspects of life – racial practices or social status – as a way of showing that what he says about sexuality and marital status is not an isolated case (7:17–24). The person who feels stuck in his marriage, or strained by the isolation of his singleness, is not in a uniquely difficult situation. The put-upon slave or the discriminated-against Jew both have their own problems to cope with, and can offer moral support and sympathy to someone coping with a difficult marriage or (we might add) the isolation of divorce. Paul adds this paragraph not just as a means of bolstering an intellectual argument, but as an encouragement to Christian understanding, sympathy and pastoral support.

In that light 7:21f., where he seems to undermine his own case, makes more sense. Paul writes with empathy for people caught in the undignified status of slavery and concedes that they may indeed long to be free from it. In this, what he says would match his concession to the divorcee. His wording is ambiguous, however. His logic seems to run: 'Stay a slave, even if you have the chance to gain freedom.' But would such a remark, tossed off casually in the course of an illustration, actually be an effective illustration of the point he wants to make? How many slaves, ex-slaves or even slave-owners in his audience would take it as a self-evident point to clinch another argument? The passage could be translated: 'Were you a slave when you were converted? Do not let that trouble you but, even if you have the opportunity to become free, prefer to bear with it. For the man who was converted as a slave is the Lord's freed-man.'[10] However the same words can be translated: 'Were you a slave when you were converted? Do not let it trouble you. (But if in fact you have the opportunity to become free, prefer to take it.) For the man . . .' If the latter translation is what Paul meant, it adds weight to his concession over divorces (though the concession does not hang upon any concession he offers slaves).

The pastoral message of the paragraph is that the grass is not necessarily greener on the other side of the fence. Our present peace of mind and moral security are more threatened by dreaming of 'if onlys' than by seeking the peace of God where we are. Divorce may solve one problem, but it creates others.

The remainder of the chapter does not bear directly on divorce, but does show more of the factors which influenced Paul's teaching. He was conscious of the crisis of the times. He expected the Lord to return in the near future. He also knew of the trials that were besetting Christians in the early days of the Church and believed that they would do so increasingly until the Lord came. Marriage ties were a liability in the event of arrest or violence and a distraction from the vital work of Christian service and evangelism. Thus Paul reckons that a person is better off single, though those who choose marriage are doing a fine thing. From this we may deduce three things: that Paul is giving advice for people within the very distinct community of the Church; that singleness for the sake of the kingdom can offer distinct advantages (and that applies in all generations); and that his conclusions were shaped in part by his conviction – over-optimistic as it has turned out – that the Lord's return would be within a few years. When the last point is removed from the equation, as it was by the second century AD, then Paul's practical advice seems to be an encouragement to the asceticism he was in fact criticizing earlier in the chapter.

A further point is that Paul, despite his honest belief that he was directed by the Spirit of God, was also drawing conclusions from his own particular experience. As a travelling missionary he knew the freedom of being single (or widowed) and how that enabled him to serve Christ more whole-heartedly than others could. As a former persecutor of the Church he had possibly seen what suffering could do when a couple were torn between their love of each other and their love of the Lord. Also, though

Jews were encouraged to remarry (at least in the case of a childless widow) because of their emphasis on the race and the land, there was in Roman society a prejudice against the widow (if not the widower) who married again, failing to observe the proper pieties for her dead husband. How much this may have influenced Paul, a Roman citizen, is difficult to assess. It is also conceivable that his own experience of marriage had left him with a jaundiced view of married life, from which he wanted to spare his readers!

Without a strong sense of the imminent return of Christ and the reality of persecution, some of what he writes does read like the views of a misogynist. However, his conscious thinking was shaped by his eschatology; as for his unconscious, he had a high view of the rights and status of women. In his dealings with women, as reported in Acts, we see someone acting confidently and graciously, with a freedom that belied his rabbinic training.

I have elaborated on the latter part of this chapter because it lies behind some of the thinking by the early Christian Fathers about remarriage after widowhood, which is in turn part of the background to their treatment of remarriage after divorce. Paul's motives in discouraging remarriage after a spouse's death were practical rather than moral ones, given his particular situation. Whatever later writers said, he thought remarriage in that situation, so long as it was 'in the Lord' (i.e. between Christians), was perfectly right and proper.

1 Timothy – 'Husband of one wife'

In laying down criteria for *episcopoi* and deacons in 1 Timothy 3 and for *presbyteroi* in Titus 1:6 Paul requires that they be 'husband of one wife' (*mias gynaikos aner*). A similar phrase is used of official widows in 1 Timothy 5:9 who cannot claim church support if they have remarried. This phrase does not directly deal with the question of remarriage after divorce, unless it is held (with no definite evidence in the text) that some of the possible candidates had been divorced as pagans and remarried. It might refer to polygamy – but this was rare, though theoretically possible; or to concubinage – not unlikely in a slave-owning household, despite commentators' dismissal of the possibility. It could mean 'monogamous – not given to affairs', but the Greek is stronger than that. Such a usage belongs to modern American psychology, not Paul!

In antiquity it was taken as ruling out remarriage after the death of the spouse, and reflects a desire that church leaders should be 'above reproach' in a society which placed a high value on such restraint from what was regarded as the indulgence of a second marriage.[11] Once again we see a concern for the Church's witness in a world which had great admiration for restraint, even though it contained examples of great licence. However once the idea had been enshrined in scripture, its motive was overlooked. It became a command which could be carried to extremes that Paul never allowed. Origen (c. 185–254 AD, orthodox though something of an extremist) thought that the twice married might be excluded from the kingdom. His contemporaries, the Montanist schismatics, actually excommunicated those who married a second time after widowhood.[12]

Conclusion

The New Testament epistles offer a positive evaluation of marriage and sexual love within it. They encourage a higher view of the place of women within the Christian community and within marriage than would have been true in contemporary society. They attempt to offer balanced advice on the Christian conduct of marriage, which errs neither in favour of the extreme asceticism nor the licence in vogue at the time. They thus favour a far more restrained approach to second marriages in general than we are familiar with in the twentieth century. In particular, divorce is acknowledged as possible, though reconciliation is the true Christian path. Opportunities for evangelism should weigh more heavily in Christian thinking about a difficult marriage than the desire for an easy time. Remarriage, it seems, is accepted at least when the former spouse is outside the Christian community. However if so, it is on the same restrained terms as any second marriage. This concession is an attempt to develop our Lord's teaching in a way that applies to new circumstances, and the motives are not simply a blind obedience to a law laid down by him.

This specific teaching is given within the wider teaching about Christian living. The same resources are available to a married Christian couple in their relationship as to any Christian in his or her dealings with others – the fruit of the Spirit which is love, joy, peace, patience, and so on; a love which bears all things, hopes all things, and keeps no score of wrongs; and gifts of the Spirit which enable them to speak the truth in love so that they grow in maturity as people and as Christians. All Christians know that Christ is the great reconciler, and that they can afford to forgive because God in Christ accepts and forgives them.

Notes

1. W. Barclay, *The Gospel of John vol. 1* (Edinburgh: St Andrews Press, 1955), p. 155, citing rabbinic stories.
2. Greg Forster, *Cohabitation and Marriage* (London: Marshall Pickering, 1994), pp. 36–9.
3. Cf. discussion and texts in John Bowman, trans. and ed., *Samaritan Documents* (Pittsburg: Pickwick Press, 1977), pp. 298–328.
4. Cf. the tractate on divorce: 'Gittin' in *The Mishnah*, H. Danby, trans. (Oxford: Oxford University Press, 1933), p. 307ff.
5. At least by the second century CE. Cf. Ketubot.4^5 (*On Marriage Contracts*). How much of the Hillel/Shammai debate was about how much dowry had to be repaid, rather than permission to divorce? Apparently Maimonides (*c.* 1135–1204 AD) believed that the 'Great Synagogue' (i.e. Ezra and his contemporaries) instituted marriage contracts, but the documents from before this date – from southern Egypt – also include such contracts. The Samaritan usage (from a group at daggers drawn with Ezra and Nehemiah) is virtually identical. This suggests they date from even before the Exile (cf. Bowman, *op. cit.*).
6. Is the emphasis on remarriage as adultery an opposition to remarriage *per se*, or a means of discouraging easy divorce by saying 'You can't instantly pair off with someone else'? What evidence is there that Jesus might think in terms of an

ontological marriage persisting beyond the phenomenological split? If he did think this way, we should think of adultery as committed against 'the marriage' rather than the people offended. But then, why does Jesus explicitly and controversially say that a husband commits adultery *against his wife*?

7. L. H. Feldman in H. Shanks, ed., *Christianity and Rabbinic Judaism* (London: SPCK, 1993), p. 29.
8. See also, most recently, A. E. Harvey, *Promise or Pretence?* (London: SCM Press, 1994), p. 20ff. Cf A. R. Winnett, *The Church and Divorce* (London: Mowbrays, 1968), chapter 1.
9. Cf. C. K. Barratt, *A Commentary on the First Epistle to the Corinthians* (London: A. & C. Black, 1968), pp. 160ff. with reference to 1 Corinthians 7:15.
10. Cf. Barratt, *op. cit.*, p. 170, with reference to 1 Corinthians 7:21ff.
11. Cf. Kelly, *The Pastoral Epistles* (London: A. & C. Black, 1963), p. 75. He notes 'On this matter, as on many others, the attitude of antiquity differed markedly from that prevalent in most circles today . . .'
12. See Clement of Alexandria, *On Marriage (Stromateis* III), Oulton and Chadwick, eds., (London: SCM Press 1953), Introduction.

FIVE

A Short History of Marriage and Divorce

The Roman world

The attitude to divorce and marriage in the Roman world forms a background to what we read in the New Testament. It is also the environment within which the Church in the first centuries of the Christian era formulated its teaching, reacting against certain features and being influenced by them. However, we need to remember the geographical range and the historical spread meant by 'the Roman world'. The available evidence is fragmentary, but we can read about the literary and ruling classes, and glean information from gravestones and the way lawyers, doctors and moralists wrote.

There were several married states in Roman law. The upper-caste (patrician) and rare *confarreatio* was supposedly indissoluble. In *matrimonium* the wife might be transfered *in manum* – into the hold – of her husband in some cases; in other cases she might retain more control of her self and her property, and run her finances almost independently of her husband's. Even these formal arrangements were not required in law. Rawson states that the commonest form of marriage involved no essential ceremonial and was based on enduring co-habitation 'accompanied by marital intention and regard', though some prior form of betrothal might be observed.[1] This applied especially to members of the non-citizen classes. For the vast numbers of slaves and ex-slaves the legal position was more tenuous still and formal marriage was not recognized. Their relationships were termed *contubernia* – tent-sharing. Despite the instability of slave relationships, which might be broken by sale or transfer, there is evidence from inscriptions that many did make great efforts to maintain their commitment to each other.

Marital relationships between people of different statuses were frowned upon and might result in the degradation of the higher-class partner. There was a great prejudice against a free woman marrying a slave, which continued well into the fourth century despite the increasingly cosmopolitan nature of Roman culture. Such prejudice seems to have found a home in some quarters of the Church. In the late second and early third centuries a presbyter in Rome called Hippolytus broke away from the mainstream Church on the grounds of its moral laxity. He criticized the Bishop of Rome, Callixtus, for allowing *contubernia* between slave men and free women and giving them, in the Church's eyes, the moral force of marriage. Hippolytus found this immoral and only allowed a Christian slave woman to live as wife with a free man on condition that she thereafter remained with the man or took no other partner. Yet he had to recognize that her slave status gave her little choice in the matter.[2] He also argued that a Christian man who had a concubine should either separate from her or marry legally, on pain of exclusion from the Church.

In upper-class society divorce seems to have been common, though Roman literature sometimes has the lurid quality of a gossip column and was often written by the upper classes themselves for their own titivation. Many, if not most, of the prominent ladies of the early Empire appear to have been divorced, some several times, but that may tell us no more about the experience of normal Romans than gossip about Hollywood stars today. The grounds for such divorces might be adultery, but equally it could be political advantage for the husband or the wife's father. Direct accusations of adultery do not seem to be common, unless there was the political motive of blackening someone's name. There was little concept of a 'guilty party', and the process was relatively informal and capable of being effected unilaterally by either party. There was no necessity to give a reason, though a wife might find difficulty in recovering her dowry in full if she initiated the separation or her husband accused her of some fault. Childlessness, which was regarded as the woman's fault, was a common reason for divorce, however, but such divorces seem to have involved no recrimination (at least not on the surface. We do not sense the inner feelings of the parties in the literature.) Children automatically reverted to the father's custody on divorce. Such society behaviour may set the tone of laxity but not reflect common practice. From a study of inscriptions and family links the foremost family historian of these times reportedly has not found much evidence of divorce among the lower classes.[3]

Roman marriage, though technically monogamous, has been called 'serial polygamy' by some students of comparative law. None the less, love and loyalty had their place in such marriages. There is one famous tombstone of a lady known as Turia. Her husband records his devotion and love for her, and hers to him, and as evidence states that she offered him divorce since she was childless. He declined the offer out of love for her. The implication of the inscription is that Turius does not intend to remarry, out of piety towards her.

In the ideology of the time, the bearing of children was highly significant. It became almost a communal paranoia among the ruling classes such that Augustus legislated for it, requiring widows under fifty to remarry within two years so as to bear children. This offended against a common sense of piety, which expected a widow to remain unmarried and to continue offering prayers for her dead husband. It appears from other tombstones that to be an *univira* – wife of one husband – was a source of pride and honour, despite the imperial legislation. In protest against Augustus' law (and to avoid it) some upper-class women in Rome apparently registered as prostitutes. While it would be anachronistic to speak of any movement for 'women's rights', such behaviour does show how some women might not easily accept a dominant male ideology which portrayed their role as loyal, chaste, domestic and subservient.[4]

There was also an ascetic strand in the ideologies of the Roman world, for all that we hear of its licence. The pagan medical writer Galen admired celibacy, while the Alexandrian

Christian teacher Clement (*c.* 155–220 AD) could argue the superiority of Christianity before a pagan philosopher audience by contrasting the passionless relationships of 'some Christians who are married but have no sexual relations with their wives' with the restrained passion of the pagan philosopher.[5] Such philosophy was fearful of 'passion', as we have seen, lest the true spiritual self became enslaved by the forces to which the physical body made it vulnerable. To conquer 'passion' was therefore a philosophic ideal which placed a high value on asceticism and abstinence. While they would reject the image of the soul entombed in the body, the thinkers in the early Church were caught in a kind of one-upmanship as they sought to demonstrate the superiority of Christianity by claiming that its marriage discipline was 'more passionless than thou'. Popular feeling among Church members may not have gone along with that, but 'although the laity continued to express their preference for married clergy, it was explained to them that they did not know what was good for them.[6] Once the idea was adopted in print it took on the inflexibility of 'the party line'.

This ascetic teaching was found among the Gnostics, who presented a challenge to the early Church. They rivalled the Church's teaching of salvation with creeds based on esoteric knowledge and ascetic or licentious practice (on the grounds that if the body was nothing, you could do what you liked with it without harming your soul). When such ideas are taken into account we can understand why Clement of Alexandria taught such a restrained view of marriage. To us he may seem excessively hard in suggesting that the second marriage of someone whose partner had died was to be avoided, though it was 'better to marry', as the lesser of two evils, 'than to burn'. However he was looking over his shoulder at even orthodox teachers like Origen, who wondered whether such people were 'of the Church' and would be excluded from the kingdom. Origen quoted 1 Timothy to support the idea that proper Christians would (like the elders of that letter) be husbands of only one wife.[7] There was a great deal of encouragement in the New

Testament for such asceticism, especially for those who retained its expectation of an imminent Second Coming or who overlooked that context altogether and took Paul's advice about avoiding marriage as a command for all time.

Clement looked back to the Lord for advice on this matter and found it in a 'gospel of the Egyptians,' which he knew was not one of the canonical four but took to be reliable on this point. Salome asks Jesus how long death will prevail on the earth, and he replies, 'So long as women bear children', which Clement takes to mean so long as passions are active in the world. 'I would have done better, then,' says Salome, 'if I had not born a child.' Jesus replies, 'Eat every food, but don't eat what you find bitter', implying to Clement that it is a matter of choice, not command, whether a person marries and bears children or not.[8] He goes on, wisely, to point out the pastoral dangers of turning proper Christian self-control into bitterness, bitterness into misanthropy and misanthropy into lack of Christian love. It is as great a danger as becoming too absorbed in one's marriage to care about others.

I have spent some time elaborating on this area of early Christian teaching because it is both a contrast and a parallel with our own agonizing about remarriage after divorce. For the early Church the problem was one which we hardly see at all today.[9] For them, witness to high moral standards was important, but it could lead to extremes of legalism and to schisms. By looking at what outsiders expected alongside the breadth of New Testament teaching the Church may well have distorted its attitude to marriage as a whole.

This distortion threatened the balance of teaching in the Latin Church also. Though positive about a first marriage, Tertullian (*c.* 160–220 AD) suggested that celibacy might be preferable and advised his wife that a chaste widowhood was second only to virginity on the scale of virtue. He even questioned the accepted importance of childbearing in the light of the expected 'time of trial', asking, 'Why should we be anxious to propagate children ... in view of the straightened times that are at hand?' He too placed a high value on continence within marriage, and regarded second marriages after bereavement as 'prejudicial to the faith and a great obstacle to holiness.'[10] As noted in Chapter 2, Augustine shaped the Western Church's thinking about marriage, but he bent the New Testament towards asceticism. He showed ambivalence towards sexual intercourse, even within marriage, yet placed a high value on the procreation of children. He regarded Christian marriage as binding, a *sacramentum*, which separation cannot undo.

The Middle Ages – sacred and secular

Augustine may have shaped the Western Christian view of marriage for the next millennium, but as an institution marriage remained secular. Church services at the time of marriage tended to be the blessing of an existing civil arrangement rather than the event which made the couple man and wife, though the Church and its courts had claimed increasing jurisdiction over marriage since the time of Tertullian. The marriage customs of the nations who overran the western Roman Empire in the fifth and sixth centuries had been similar to those of ancient Rome, namely monogamy, with fairly easy divorce obtainable by either party as they wished.[11]

This attitude to divorce dominated the Dark Ages, but Christian standards came to be applied between the tenth and thirteenth centuries. During the Middle Ages Church lawyers made their influence felt, so that alongside the clearly 'church' marriage (at the church porch followed by a nuptial mass) they succeeded in 'baptizing' customary practice, private pledges and family contracts to which the couple were party under the headings of *verba de praesenti* and *verba de futuro*. Cynics may say that this was just the lawyers extending their monopoly; those of a more generous mind might say that they were enforcing the benefits and security of a Christian view of marriage on a populace which might otherwise discard each other wantonly.[12] In the event, a theoretically high view of the permanence of marriage came to prevail which broke down the casual attitude towards its dissolution. However, such a theory of marriage was very rigid. Hard-hearted human beings find such rigidity difficult to live with. Like Moses (cf. Mark 10:5) they look for allowances!

One feature of the Church's teaching on marriage was that within forbidden degrees it was sinful and a potential moral danger. The forbidden degrees came to be counted not just in blood relationships but also through affinity and gossipry – i.e. relationships contracted through godparents and godchildren. At one period in the early Middle Ages these were counted to the seventh degree though eventually this contracted to the fourth (of affinity though not of blood kindred) as the system was found to be unworkable. Such extensions of the biblical restrictions may seem laughable, but they were taken seriously. There is a story from Italy of a man who took his own child back from the priest at its baptism – an action that implied godparenthood – and then faced uncertainty as to whether he could still remain married to his wife, since she could not be married to her child's godfather!

The effect of all this was that it became relatively easy to argue that an apparently permanent and indissoluble marriage had in fact never been a valid marriage at all. In a close-knit community some hitherto unremembered relationship might be found which could justify the *divortium a vinculo matrimonii* of the couple (the annulment of the marriage, with the proviso that any children would be treated as born in good faith and so legitimate). If no tie of blood, marriage or gossipry were found, some other impediment might be alleged, such as a pre-contract to marry another, lack of proper consent, or non-consummation (a strong possibility if children had been married young to cement some bond between noble families). There are a number of such cases in the history of European royalty. The popular literature of the day might encourage easy dismissal of a spouse with tales of spurious edification in which, for example, a prince dismisses his devoted, pagan (e.g. Spanish Muslim) wife to take up with a 'nice Christian girl'. The official ideology was also somewhat ambivalent about the relative value of marriage, so that the union between Abelard and Eloise could be forced apart on the grounds of his lesser orders, despite its celebration in church by a priest. MacFarlane also notes that a couple seeking such 'divorce' needed to have funds to pay the lawyers.

The overall effect was to make the permanence of marriage somewhat uncertain. Major cases or those with complications, such as Henry VIII's, were referred to the Pope, but diocesan courts could handle less serious matters. There was an obvious double standard here, whatever the annulment rate actually was, and it was one of the abuses of Church power that the reformers chose to set straight in the sixteenth century. The Church's approach did, however, allow very high ideals to be upheld at the same time as recognizing the frailties of human nature and the vagaries of affection. But it was a legal fiction and so brought the system into disrepute as the Church was caught between the logic of doctrines pushed to their extremes and a need to recognize the pastoral situation.

Marriage and sacrament

Before turning to developments after the Reformation, it is worth considering the idea of marriage as a sacrament. It was a development which, as will become clear, I believe was misguided. The belief that marriage ought to be a lifelong permanent commitment or that there is a quality in such commitment which reflects the commitment of God to his people is laudable. If that was all that the word 'sacrament' meant when applied to marriage, then I should be happy to use it for that is what I believe is said in our Lord's discussions of marriage and divorce and in Paul's letter to the Ephesians. However, the word 'sacrament' has additional connotations which distort what was intended in those passages. The misuse of sacramental terminology and the consequent distortion of pastoral support for those who find their marriages difficult or broken has not been a positive outcome. However, in its time, the use of sacramental language had a positive function. I believe that we should look for some equivalent means of encouraging the permanence of marriage that is appropriate to our age.

The use of the word 'sacrament' in connection with marriage has a long history, complicated by the development of sacramental theology as a whole. The formal declaration that marriage was one of the seven sacraments of Catholic tradition did not in fact come until 1439. When the Roman scholar St Jerome came to translate the New Testament into Latin at the turn of the fourth century CE he rendered the Greek *musterion* as *sacramentum* in three of its four occurrences in Ephesians, including 5:32. In this text St Paul, as we have seen, was highlighting the analogy between Christ's love for his people, and a husband's love for his wife. The original meaning of the word *sacramentum* was 'sacred commitment' or 'vow', but it had a secondary meaning of 'sacred rite' which does coincide with *musterion* in Greek, so that this was a fair rendering of what was by then a Christian technical term. Augustine (Epistles 138) defined *sacramentum* by saying, 'signs, when they apply to divine matters, are called *sacramenta*', and elsewhere he calls baptism and the blood of Christ 'sacramenta'. Nevertheless, in using the word in his discussion of marriage, Augustine was stressing its permanence, not its mystical nature. Just as the Roman soldier was bound to his commander by his oath, hallowed by imprecation to the gods (*sacramentum*), so in Christian marriage here was a vow which committed the couple to each other securely.[13] (He also compared it with the indelibility of priestly orders.) The link was made between the pledge of marriage and the signs inherent in baptism and the Lord's supper. Thus from the quirk in Jerome's translation of a Pauline analogy and Augustine's position as the major theological writer in Western Europe has grown an extensive doctrinal superstructure which shaped the discussion of marriage within the Catholic church until the Reformation.

Consideration of the way in which thought about the prime sacrament – the Lord's supper – developed will illustrate how marriage and divorce moved from being simply a moral issue into being a matter of essential and sacramental realities. The

Jewish Passover was (and is) an act of remembrance, by which participants identify themselves with their origins. It is as if they are there at the Exodus. They also identify themselves with their nation and its history, good and ill, down 3,000 years or so. In using and changing the Passover so that it represented his death, Jesus was inviting his followers to identify themselves with him and what he was to do for them. The *matzah* (bread) and wine did not become his body or blood any more than they became the bread of affliction that had been eaten in Egypt. Taking and eating or drinking them were symbols of his followers' moral choice to side with him through his new Exodus into his new Israel. The tangible actions of eating and drinking signified a real commitment in the physical world.

When this holy meal was taken out of its Jewish and historic context and transposed into a Hellenistic pattern of thought – in which reality was spiritual and out of this world, and in which what we see in this world reflects a greater reality in an ideal world above – then it became natural to think of the bread and wine as tokens on earth of an eternal reality in heaven. They and those who share them, partake of that reality and are an earthly representation of it. This transposition came early in Christian history and there are signs of such thinking beginning in Hebrews and 2 Peter (though it is not applied there to the Lord's supper or baptism). At this stage in its development, however, it does not seriously distort the significance of the Eucharist to see it as a participation in the eternal Christ.

When, by the double associations of the word *sacramentum*, marriage came to be looked upon in this light, a distortion was introduced. A marriage on earth somehow became a participation in an ideal, heavenly union, which had a reality over and above the practical partnership on earth. Whereas Christ had spoken of the moral imperative of not breaking up the God-given union of marriage, there was now, it seemed, an eternal reality in existence which could not be dissolved, even where adultery or separation had disrupted the earthly union.

By the later Middle Ages, the concept of heavenly realities and their earthly reflections became less dominant in people's thought, to be replaced by a greater concentration on physical substance. At this point a further distortion took place. In the Eucharist, people looked not so much at the eternal reality (*substantia*) that it represented as at what it had become on earth. In marriage, people asked what was the physical fact that gave marriage its substance. Somewhat uneasily, in the light of what had gone before, some saw it in its consummation. Others focused on the consent or the Church's blessing, so that the shift away from morality towards mystique was not so great as with the Eucharist. The idea persisted, however, that there could be a reality in existence other than that which was an observable physical or social fact on the altar or in the broken household. In the Eucharist the words are the same: 'This is the bread of affliction', 'This is my body given for you.' Their meaning has been changed by a double shift in thought forms. In marriage, too, the words are unchanged – 'Let not man divide' – but the grammatical mood is understood not as imperative but as indicative: man cannot divide, not because it is not God's moral will, but because there is some indissoluble reality created by the couple's 'I will'. Yet even as he explained his Father's moral will, Christ recognized that not everyone would be able to take it and keep it. Thus I believe that the shift from morals to metaphysics has distorted Christ's pastoral application of his moral ideals.

The Reformation and beyond

If the rigidity of the ancient Church's teaching was in part due to its historical circumstances, the next development in England is a matter of historical accident. England inherited from Roman canon law at the Reformation a view that marriage was inherently indissoluble. Divorce as we know it was not permitted – though it could be argued at that time that a marriage, such as Henry VIII's to Catherine of Aragon (see Appendix I), had never existed and so the couple might legitimately part and remarry. The Reformers reacted strongly against the earlier abuse of nullity. Annulments became rare, and the accepted grounds were far narrower than those in the unreformed mediaeval Church: a prior commitment (through betrothal or espousal) to another partner, consanguinity within the relationships found in Leviticus (i.e. in the Bible, not tradition), and male impotence over a three-year period. If one partner disappeared for over seven years death was presumed, and remarriage permitted. (Hence the significance in many of our folk-songs of someone returning after seven years to find a betrothed still faithful.) Separation of bed and board might be obtained from the ecclesiastical courts in each diocese (where jurisdiction remained until the legislative reforms of 1857). The grounds for such separation were excessive cruelty or adultery. The process would include a financial settlement worked out between families and 'friends' acting as go-betweens. This was spoken of as divorce in current parlance. However, it was not at first clear whether this carried with it the permission to remarry implicit in divorce today – a case under Edward VI allowed remarriage, and in Elizabeth's reign this precedent was accepted without any clear legislation until it was reversed in the canons of 1603.

Legal practices

The English Reformation initially failed to legislate for those who were formally separated because of cruelty or adultery. Cranmer was working on the issue in 1552 at the time of Edward VI's death, and would have allowed divorce (with remarriage) on grounds not only of adultery but also of desertion, deadly hostility and prolonged ill-treatment. This proposal lapsed with the accession of Mary and Cranmer's execution, and was not revived by Elizabeth, though the courts appear to have presumed it informally.[14] There are instances during the reigns of Elizabeth I and James I when bishops granted licences for the remarriage of such 'divorced' parties, but the law was not clear. In the 1603 canons, however, the situation was clarified. Remarriage of 'divorced' persons was now forbidden, though even after the canons were promulgated Bishop (as he then was)

Laud did grant a licence and in 1605 himself remarry a guilty party. The Bigamy Act of 1603 apparently exempted parties to such a wedding from penalty, though bigamy itself was a capital offence. (These canons specified the manner of marriage ceremonies, producing the quirk that a marriage conducted in breach of the rules was illegal and yet valid and binding for life! Such an irregular marriage, even by a clerk in holy orders, might well be regarded as easily dissoluble by one or both parties, as Shakespeare's Touchstone suggests in *As You Like It* '. . . he is not like to marry me well, and not being well married it will be a good excuse hereafter for me to leave my wife' (III, iii, 80ff.).

Other Reformed churches made allowance for the remarriage of separated persons. Scotland allowed divorce for adultery or desertion from the date of its Reformation, with remarriage permitted to the innocent party. Martin Bucer argued for divorce on the grounds of a conviction for serious crime, impotence, leprosy or insanity, as well as on the more general Reformation view that desertion as well as adultery justified divorce.[15] Despite a debate that continued among the bishops until the 1630s, England and its Church was left with a régime even more rigid than Roman canon law, which allowed annulment for more reasons. It was the only Reformation country which ended up with no clear provision for divorce and remarriage.

For those who wished to remarry, perhaps because a legitimate heir was important, the only recourse was a private Act of Parliament, which was expensive and by no means sure. There were 131 instances between 1669 and 1799, and only seventeen successful Bills before 1750. The first such private Act was passed for Lord de Roos in 1669. The next Act was not until twenty-three years later, for the Duke of Norfolk, and there were only three more before the accession of the Hanoverian kings.[16] The bishops do not appear to have raised theological objections in the House of Lords to these Acts, though attempts were made to stop the second marriages of guilty parties. Stone quotes the case of Sir George Downing in 1701, who had contracted an arranged marriage when he and his bride were both fifteen. The marriage was apparently not then consummated, and soon afterwards he left to go abroad for four years. The couple never lived together thereafter. Parliament turned down his request for an Act of divorce by the narrow margin of forty-nine votes to forty-seven. The argument that carried the day was that both parties were of an age to give consent. It is significant that Parliament presumed such a flimsy marriage to exist and that, despite the Enlightenment, the mediaeval lawyers' question of consent carried the argument, rather than pragmatic matters such as separation or even the non-consummation of the marriage.

Such divorces by Act of Parliament were rarely obtained by women. The first was in 1801, and there were only four prior to 1857. Though initially it was titled or landed gentry who obtained them, it was not limited to such persons and there were cases effected by clerks and salesmen. The median cost (as assessed when law reform was mooted in the 1850s) was £475 – which was no small sum, but still less than has been alleged.[17]

Related developments

Two other developments in the legal circumstances of marriage should be noted at this point. Firstly, in 1753 Lord Hardwicke's Act imposed a very strict requirement that the only valid marriage in England and Wales (except for Quakers and Jews, who themselves kept full records) was to be one conducted in Church of England churches after proper legal notice had been given. The proponents of this Act regarded it as a victory for Reason over superstition. Allowance was made for other churches in subsequent legislation, but the various forms of common law marriage, either by some ceremony, or by custom and repute, were made invalid even if they lingered in popular thought.[18] Secondly, in what may be regarded as a further step towards the secularization of society, provision was made in 1837 for civil registration of marriages. Registration and the increasing bureaucratization of the country are relevant to this story. If the uncertain course of the Reformation had left

England and its Church with an exceedingly rigid law on divorce and remarriage, the tighter record-keeping as well as the propriety of the Victorians brought that rigidity home to all levels of society.

Informal arrangements

That was the legal position, which would apply to those for whom the law was important. However, little could be done, other than by public opinion, to keep a couple together if one or both wished otherwise and they had no fixed property or name to preserve. Stone refers to a census in Norwich in 1570, in which 8 per cent of those categorized 'poor' were wives of men who had disappeared.[19] In a later book he has changed his mind and suggests that at the end of the Middle Ages England was not a separating or divorcing society. As the population became more mobile, the effectiveness of banns (if they were used) in preventing bigamy after desertion became minimal. A folk song from Ireland expresses the situation admirably;

> ... 'twas there I fell a courting
> with a hansom young fellow, had a wife of his own.
> He said he would take me, and never forsake me,
> and after some time we could get married
> where there's none to know.[20]

The actual frequency of such bigamous marriages is difficult to assess. The infrequency of prosecutions may mean that few people were caught, few communities objected enough to act, or few actual instances occurred. There were cases of sailors or wanderers in the American colonies who had a wife in every port – but were such cases regular occurrences, or sufficiently salacious to make the headlines even then? Desertion was certainly common enough for dreams of the returning wanderer to prove an attractive theme in folk song, such as 'Spencer the Rover' (which dates from a time when a 'clear fountain' might be found 'at Yorkshire, near Rotherham'!). The rover departed for financial problems – 'he had been so reduced' – and his return 'so surprised' his children and wife 'to see such a stranger once more in their sight.'[21]

Where husband and wife were in agreement about their separation, there was in popular belief a further means of effecting a 'divorce'. The husband would lead his wife in a halter to a recognized market, and would proceed to offer her for sale as if she were cattle, perhaps even paying a fee to the clerk of the market. She would then be sold to an appropriate bidder, and all the parties would retire to an inn to celebrate. The bidder might well have been arranged beforehand – a lover perhaps. He now took responsibility for his new wife. In the popular eye her former husband was freed of his duties to her, though legally such a transaction had no validity. Evidence for this practice is at its most common in the eighteenth century, and the last recorded case dates from 1887. However, its roots are in the mediaeval period, if not earlier, from an era when custom and common law, not canon law, governed marriage and separation.[22]

Another 'common law divorce' ritual existed alongside customary rites of marriage: Phillips writes of couples who married over the brush (literally) – by together jumping across the threshold over a brush balanced between the doorposts and without touching it. Their union might be reversed by reversing the symbolism: they had to jump backwards out of the house over the brush.[23] In the Welsh examples he refers to, this would be recognized by the community (though not necessarily approved of) if it were done within a year of the marriage, and was appropriate for cases of incompatibility or infertility. Such rituals publicized the severance of the couple's relationship, and invited public acceptance of the fact. No doubt the physical difficulty of jumping backwards within a narrow space meant that they would not act too hastily!

In more settled districts a sanction existed for wives who were being ill-treated and were supported by public opinion. 'Rough music' was a means of embarrassing an errant husband into improving his behaviour. The wife's sympathizers gathered outside the man's home, beating pots and pans and generally taunting him for his unfaithfulness or violence. In the absence of protection from the courts, and legal aid, this gave the victim of violence or injustice some protection and support from her society. Such customs did not always favour the 'victim' however. A bullied or cuckolded husband might also be the victim of rough music. His ineffectuality in guarding his rights, it was felt, undermined everyone else's marriage!

Women's status

Also relevant to this picture of marriage and divorce in the century before reform is the legal status of wives and children. It was the father's prerogative to have custody of his children if the couple separated, however unsuitable he might be. A formal deed could provide otherwise. On his death, his wife need not be appointed their legal guardian. This was tempered by legislation in 1839.

A married woman was not a separate person in law but could only conduct business as an extension of her husband. Thus, unless a formal separation deed giving details of a financial settlement had been drawn up, perhaps with the aid of family or friends as intermediaries, a separated woman earning her own living might, in an extreme case, find that living sequestered at source by her husband. Of course, she might counter by running up debts for which *he* was liable! From gentry and clergy to shopkeepers, industrious women might find their efforts squandered by extravagant husbands against whom they had little recourse, even when separated. An attempt to remedy this situation – made by a Member of Parliament, T. E. Parry, during the 1850s – was met with scorn and vitriol in Parliament and the press. Polite society was reluctant to recognize violence or even sexuality within marriage, not to mention the economic freedom or the separate personhood of the wife. (The learned clerics who edited Augustine's treatise *On the Good of Marriage* in 1847[24] felt they had to preface its restrained language with a 'health warning', and urged readers to put aside their 'modern delicacy' and let their 'minds be strengthened against evil suggestions by seeing the whole subject as a field of Christian duty'!) The Government promised legislation about women's property, but merely safeguarded separated wives' earnings in the Divorce Act that followed. Married women still lacked personhood before the law. A partial solution in the Married Women's Property Act of 1870 left women trading in their own right, unable to obtain credit, until more thoroughgoing reform in 1882.

Until 1891 it was held that common law allowed a husband forcibly to detain his wife if she attempted to leave him – and to beat her by way of correction. Perkin suggests that it was the recognition of women's independent personality in law in 1870 that worried men more than the divorce reforms of thirteen years earlier: 'Few men seek divorce, but many have wives!'[25] Women left in other ways too, however. The average life expectancy and length of marriages is significant. Many women died young, in childbirth or because of related stresses, and Perkin suggests the average length for a nineteenth-century marriage was fourteen years. Stone calculates that of the marriages that took place in 1826, 30 per cent had ended through the death of one or both parties within twenty years; the same percentage of 1980 marriages will end in the same length of time through divorce.[26]

Though we may not be aware of this background, it is in reaction to it that reform has taken place over the past 150 years. Perhaps the most significant point is how the clerics in 1847 so easily saw the institution of marriage as one of *duty*, in contrast to late twentieth-century thinking that '*love* changes everything'.

Reform of divorce law – 1857 onwards

It was not until 1857, in England, that divorce as we now understand it – i.e. a permanent separation with licence to marry a third party, granted by a court of law rather than an Act of Parliament – came into being. The grounds for divorce were unchanged, though many observers felt that the principle of indissolubility had been set aside. Civil judges took over the functions of the ecclesiastical courts (which were being stripped of their civil powers at that time) in what was now termed 'judicial separation' (the old divorce of bed and board). This might be granted to a man or woman, without discrimination, for adultery, cruelty or for the new 'offence' of desertion for two years. The new power for a court to dissolve the marriage absolutely was created. The man could obtain that divorce on simple grounds of adultery, but the wife had to prove cruelty, desertion or sexual aberrations in addition. Divorce might be refused if the petitioner had committed adultery or been the one to desert his or her spouse initially.

Collusion could also frustrate the petition. In 1860 the interval between the decrees nisi and absolute was introduced, not to facilitate a *rapprochement*, but for evidence of collusion or the petitioner's own matrimonial offences to be produced. It seems strange now, and not a little vindictive, that a couple who recognized that their marriage had fallen apart and were co-operating to enable each other to make a new start could be prevented from divorcing, while a contested divorce might be forced upon an unwilling party. What also seems strange from a Christian viewpoint is that if the offended party delayed taking action, that might be taken as evidence that she accepted and condoned the offence so that a petition could be refused. Thus an unsuccessful attempt at the Christian virtues of reconciliation and forgiveness would vitiate a later divorce. This had previously been the rule in the ecclesiastical courts too. Contrast this to the requirement (in theory) in the 1969 legislation that reconciliation should be mooted, and to the most recent proposals that couples should seek conciliation to come to mutually agreed settlements.

In the 1857 legislation a 'co-respondent' would be cited and might find himself paying costs and damages. Under this legislation (and until 1937) there would be a co-respondent since the grounds for divorce were adultery alone or with additional aggravations. Thus the law could be held to be within the unreformed Christian parameters which held no divorce to be possible 'except in the case of adultery'.

Over the next seventy years legislation gave added protection to women who were victims of violence, drunkenness or their husband's criminality or desertion. Publicity was restricted. Legislation also gave increasing access for 'the poor' to marital courts, by decentralizing the hearings and simplifying procedures. Nevertheless, divorce remained a comparatively rare procedure. Not until 1918 did the rate of divorces granted rise to more than 1,000 per year – perhaps as a result of wartime infidelities – though the number of formal separations was about 10,000. These were favoured by 'the poor' because they were cheaper and handled by local magistrates rather than a London court. In the early 1930s perhaps 2–3,000 cases per annum might be heard.[27] Divorce was viewed not as a right to be claimed, but as a 'relief' granted to those whose own conduct deserved it, and who could not tolerate their errant spouse's conduct.

Between 1910 and 1912 a Royal Commission sat to consider divorce. Their conclusions were not implemented immediately, partly because of World War I and partly because they were disputed: three of its members, including the Archbishop of York, submitted a minority report. In 1923 the non-controversial element of the report was enacted extending nullity to include mental illness or venereal disease unknown to the other party, and allowing women to petition on the same grounds as men – i.e. on grounds of simple adultery. The courts, however, became suspicious when it was apparent that some husbands were contriving to be caught in hotels with another woman.

Not until 1937 did Parliament implement the Commission's other recommendations, and then through the Private Member's Bill of A. P. Herbert. This enabled divorce on the grounds of cruelty, desertion (for three years) or insanity (adjudged incurable after five years). Three years had to elapse after the wedding before proceedings could begin.

Though by this legislation the reasons for divorce had been

widened (thus following long-established practice in non-Catholic countries), the basic approach remained that of relieving an 'innocent party' from the pain of a 'marital offence'. To obtain the divorce a specific fault had to be proven. A 'guilty party' who, say, deserted his wife could not take action against her, and could not force her to take action against him if for moral, or perhaps financial, social or vindictive reasons she chose not to act and herself remained celibate. One result of the Herbert Act was that divorces rose to about 7,500 a year as more people became eligible.

The Herbert Act remained in force in England and Wales until 1971. During that thirty-year period the number of divorces rose fivefold. In 1958 26,239 petitions were filed and 22,654 decrees absolute granted; and in 1966 46,609 petitions and 39,067 decrees. Even then most were undefended. The peak figures were in 1947, in the aftermath of the war, when 48,501 new petitions were filed and 60,254 decrees granted, including cases started in previous years. The instability of wartime, with its separations and infidelities, made divorce more acceptable, though greater awareness of the far more liberal American practice (through films and servicemen stationed in Britain) may have contributed. In the years before World War II, there were roughly a hundred times more divorces per annum in the USA than in England and Wales. As early as 1947 the later Lord Denning could allege that 'Some young people approach marriage with the feeling that if it does not work out, well, they can always get a divorce.'

While the raw figures suggest how attitudes are influenced, they do not always present a complete picture. For instance, between 1955 and 1960 in England and Wales the rate of divorces per thousand marriages fell from 2.4 to 2.0, though it rose again over the next five years. A larger, longer-lived population and a lowering of the normal age of marriage meant that between 1900 and 1965 both the married population and the average length of a marriage doubled. Choose statistics carefully, and you can argue anything! Whilst divorce numbers are easily defined and collected, the number of broken homes with partners unofficially separated or simply unhappy homes with partners held together by economic necessity is more difficult to collate. Stone notes a twentyfold increase in divorces between 1900 and 1957, but only a fivefold increase in the numbers of separations and divorces together.[28] Relevant factors in the rise of divorce in Britain (though perhaps not in the States) are the development of the welfare state since 1947 and the greater availability of Legal Aid in divorce cases since 1948.

Church reactions to reform

The 1857 Act had been part of a general disempowering of Church courts but nevertheless attracted some ecclesiastical support. Bishop Tait (1811–82) approved, pointing out that it reaffirmed Church practice and removed the cost and erratic nature of private Acts of Parliament. Others, such as Bishop Wilberforce (1805–73), whose well-known opposition to Darwinism suggests that he saw more clearly the creeping threat of 'modern thinking' to traditional Church values, wished to retain Christ's prohibition of divorce as a binding part of the law of the land. John Keble's (1792–1866) opposition is also notable for it is a precursor of Anglo-Catholic reaction over the next century. He recognized the growing division between Church and State implied by the legislation and argued that marriages blessed in heaven are indissoluble.

As the number of divorces rose (though at this time it was still miniscule) this was seen as a challenge to the Christian doctrine of marriage. Though the 1857 Act allowed a clergyman not to take the marriage service of a divorcee himself, he had to make the parish church available for another minister to conduct the wedding. The 1888 Lambeth Conference of Anglican bishops sought to bar the remarriage of the guilty party in parish churches. By 1908 it held remarriage in church was 'undesirable', even for the innocent party. In 1920 the word 'indissoluble' was used by the Lambeth Conference to describe 'our Lord's principle and standard', and in 1930 the Conference attempted to bar all remarriages in church and required that admission to communion, even for the innocent party, should be a matter for the bishop of the diocese.

This progression reflects the growing influence in the Anglican Church of the Anglo-Catholic movement (with communion becoming a more significant part of regular worship) and its desire to apply Roman moral theology to the pastoral practice of the Church. It also reflects the growing perception of divorce as a threat to established morality and family stability. I suggest that it shows, as part of the general tenor of the Oxford Movement, a symbolic (and possibly unconscious) attempt to assert the Church's power and influence in those areas of society where it could enforce its will at a time when its place in society at large was declining. This suggestion is difficult to prove, but it tallies with the way in which 'marriage' and 'the family' serve as symbols (as well as real agents) of security in a fast-changing world. We see this also in contemporary – 1990s – political rhetoric about 'family values' and calls from within or without for the Church to 'do something' about moral decline, by which is meant sexual morals and family structures. (These calls are often from the same people who will rubbish the Church's contribution to debates about corporate morality and social justice.) This suggestion is not without support, however. Perkin sees the growth of the authoritarian patriarchal family in the sixteenth and seventeenth centuries as a counterbalance to the loss of the order and stability that had been provided by the pre-Reformation authority of the Church.[29] The patriarchal family was used by the theorists of the divine right of kings in the seventeenth century, and the French aristocracy in the eighteenth, to reinforce their positions. And the writers of the 1988 Church of England report *An Honourable Estate* speak of the value of marriage as establishing Victorian respectability.[30]

The Oxford Movement was not the only influence on Church thinking about divorce in the nineteenth and early twentieth centuries. F. D. Maurice (1805–72) was greatly concerned about the Churches' response to the social conditions of the time and saw the advantage of the new divorce laws in freeing the Church from legalism. In connection with Jesus' own teaching, those who accepted the new 'higher criticism' of the Bible argued that the 'Matthean exception' was not from Jesus' own lips. Some took this to justify the indissolubilist position still further; others argued that Jesus had not intended his words legalistically in the first place but as moral advice, and drew on contemporary conclusions about Jesus' person and ministry to support their case. The compassion of the Jesus of History inspires different responses from the mandate of the Lord of Glory. Some of the evidence from churchmen to the 1910 Royal Commission focused on the hardship caused to one spouse by the insanity, drunkenness and cruelty of the other. They sided with those advocating change, despite the promise 'for better or worse'.

As pressure for the reform that became the Herbert Act grew, the Church of England held its own investigation into divorce and remarriage which reported to the York and Canterbury Convocations in 1934. The different approaches within the Church to divorce were apparent, with the majority coming down for indissolubility 'save by death'. A minority recognized this as an ideal but urged compassionate consideration of the troubles arising from a failure to live up to the ideal, and called on the Church to be generous to the innocent party. The Herbert Act of 1937 ultimately severed the link between civil divorce and the 'Matthean exception'. In deference to Church opposition Mr Herbert retained the relief to clergy from their common law obligation to marry anyone in their parish (first included with reference to the guilty party in 1857) if the person was divorced. In the following year the Convocations of York and Canterbury, despite the minority pleas of 1934, passed resolutions requiring clergy not to remarry divorced persons. These affirmed that 'the church should not allow the use of the marriage service in the case of anyone who has a former partner still living . . .' and that divorce and remarriage 'always involves a departure from the principle of marriage . . . as a lifelong obligation.' This affirmation was indissolubilist in effect, though its wording was milder. It put moral pressure on clergy and opened the way to episcopal censure of those who did not conform. It could not remove their legal right to take the wedding of a divorcee. These resolutions and Mr Herbert's Act came in the wake of the royal abdication brought about by King Edward's desire to marry a multiple-divorcée. As late as 1957, when the state was establishing a Royal Commission to reconsider divorce law after a failed Bill to allow it simply after seven years' separation, irrespective of guilt or innocence, these resolutions were declared to be Acts of Convocation. This added to their moral force, but did not alter their legal effect.

The Church did not want, however, to ask Parliament to approve a new canon which would be binding. Such a course might not succeed since it would seem to restrict an Act of Parliament itself. A new canon – a clause in the Church's self-regulatory legislation – had been considered at the time of the post-war surge in the divorce rate. The 1948 Lambeth Conference skirted round indissolubilist language as it discussed marriage and reaffirmed its predecessors' opinions, but it allowed the possibility that relationships had occurred where no true marriage bond existed. The draft canon of 1947 allowed a diocesan bishop and his chancellor (ecclesiastical judge) to consider whether a civil divorce might, in the Church's eyes, be considered nullity. This canon would have required Parliamentary approval, and might be deemed an attempt by the Church to tell the courts of the land that they were wrong. It also required a great deal of legal machinery, which the Church of England does not have. This draft canon did, however, show a recognition that the prevailing Anglican discipline over divorce and remarriage was most rigid, and perhaps also further reflected an admiration for the Roman system.

It was not just the bishops who were taking this hard-line approach to divorce. Winnett quotes a debate during the Chelmsford diocesan conference of 1947[31]. The remarriage of innocent parties was opposed by 357 votes to 81, as was their participation in communion for at least two years after the divorce (by the narrower margin of 189 votes to 188). Perhaps the members of that conference, and the bishops as well, recognized that the dichotomy between guilty and innocent party was too simple to convey the truth behind the breakup of a marriage, and that the 'innocent' party must bear some of the responsibility. No doubt many of them wished to affirm their obedience to Christ's commands. But the distinction between command and moral advice from the Son of God is a fine one, not easily debated or voted upon. Perhaps they felt that a vote in favour of remarrying 'innocent' divorcees would be misunderstood, even by the media of the 1940s, and might be portrayed as the Church condoning adultery. That is an ever-present risk in such debates. However, such an exclusion of the 'innocent' party is further evidence that divorce was seen as a symbol of moral decay, as a contagion that might contaminate those who came into contact with it.

Such a rejection of the divorcee can work at the level of taboo, rather than morality, and has made a deep impression in the consciousness of churchgoers and non-churchgoers alike. Even today, the divorced may feel that they have to explain themselves in a new parish, or fear the response when they ask for their children's baptism. This is not to deny that moral questions are relevant, but the way divorce has been singled out, as the offence which makes lepers of its victims, owes as much to social forces and fears as to Christian morality. Though this taboo can sometimes result in unChristian treatment of those who have been divorced, it draws upon a unconscious realization of the damage that family breakup can do to the individuals concerned and its consequences for society at large. In 1947 such a realization can only have been supported by anecdotal evidence. In 1968, Winnett can comment: 'Little evidence exists to determine whether greater harm is done to children by the divorce of their parents or by the quarrels of those who continue living together', though he adds that 'either way the children suffer'. Only in the 1980s and 1990s have research projects attempted to measure such damage in terms of education, health and public order.

Divorce law reform, 1969

In view of the disquiet within the Church of England at the development of divorce and remarriage, it is surprising that the next significant step in altering the divorce laws in England was aided and abetted, if not prompted, by a Church report. In the mid-1960s a group chaired by Robert Mortimer, Bishop of Exeter, was convened with the specific task of offering a Christian perspective on the state's regulation of divorce. This was not a study on the Church's own teaching and discipline, but an attempt to suggest how marriage might be supported and divorce regulated in a nation which was basically Christian in heritage, but by no means entirely Christian, and where people ordered their relationships under secular as well as religious influences. Their report, entitled *Putting Asunder*,[32] came out in 1966 and was controversial in departing from the hitherto accepted principle of 'marital offences' as the grounds for divorce. Instead, the group suggested that the courts ask whether a marriage had broken down irretrievably, for whatever reason – a suggestion first mooted by John Milton in the 1640s. They also proposed that the court investigate whether the couple's or an individual's claim that the marriage had broken down was correct, and whether there was hope of re-establishing the relationship soundly. They departed from the apparent biblical principle that only some sort of fault – notably adultery – could justify divorce, and seemed to allow that the death *of the marriage* might part the couple. However, they brought into play another biblical principle, that of reconciliation, which earlier legislation had vitiated because it seemed to condone the offence. They were also trying to take into account the complexities of a relationship in which one party might act disloyally or cruelly, but the other could equally be difficult to live with or subtly taunting. They were not saying 'there is no guilt in breaking up a marriage', but rather that the courts could not rebuild marriages by asking one party to demonstrate the other's guilt. They actually wanted to avoid defining grounds on which a marriage had broken down because this would merely become a new battleground for the lawyers.

Their fears were proved right in the way the 1969 legislation developed. The Law Commission felt that detailed judicial inquiry into the reasons for the breakdown of the marriage was too demanding on the courts' time and no more likely to get at the truth than the old system, particularly if the parties did not wish it to come out. Being lawyers, they also wanted specific evidence when deciding if a marriage had broken down. Thus old matrimonial offences were brought back in a different guise as facts which would demonstrate the breakdown. They were: adultery, which the petitioner could not tolerate; unreasonable behaviour; desertion over two years; separation for two years with the respondent's consent to the divorce; and separation for five years even without the respondent's consent. The court's duty was to inquire into the facts, rather than into the brokenness of the relationship, and if they were proven and the marriage did not appear retrievable, then the divorce would be granted. Solicitors acting for the parties were required to certify whether they had discussed the possibility of reconciliation, but even if the answer was no there was to be no sanction. Even *Putting Asunder* had recognized that steps towards reconciliation could not be forced upon a couple. In practice, therefore, though the Bishop of Exeter's report had proved a catalyst for reform, its main aims were frustrated by the lawyers' need for tangible evidence and the sheer workload on the divorce courts.

Initially, as with the previous legislation, no proceedings could be started within the first three years of marriage, but modifications brought this period down to one year. Further modifications to the procedure meant that the details of the case could be dealt with by post, with no real inquiry in an undefended and uncomplicated case. This leads, *de facto*, to divorce on demand, which negates the affirmation made in Church and

State weddings that marriage is a lifelong and binding union. It also leads to perceived injustices, for a respondent who may not wish to contest a divorce can find himself accused of 'unreasonable conduct' on the flimsiest of grounds. For example, a taxi-driver who works mostly at night, when fares want his services, so as to earn the family's keep finds himself divorced for being out every night. If his wife makes such an allegation, the marriage has almost certainly broken down but the reason was more profound than the fact alleged, and the lawyer who drew up the wife's petition has exploited the system rather than aided an honest inquiry.

Parallel developments

Just as the early reforms of divorce law were connected to questions of the custody of children and women's rights and freedoms, so other laws and provisions affect the modern law. Custody of children does not now necessarily go with the 'innocent' party, but is assessed on the children's best interests. The Children Act of 1989 prefers to speak of 'residence' and 'responsibility' for the children. Unless contact with the non-resident parent is deemed dangerous it is encouraged, though in practice it is often lost. Responsibility for children includes financial maintenance. Recently, and controversially, the management of this has moved from the courts to the impersonal bureaucracy of the Child Support Agency (CSA). At one level, this is the next stage in a process begun in 1857 when jurisdiction over divorce was delegated from Parliament to the courts. At a more sinister level, it represents a derogation of personal negotiation and responsibility found in the legal system to a mechanistic process devoid of human touch and sensitivity. It has not escaped critics of this development that the chief beneficiary, if the new system works as intended, will be the Treasury and not those expecting financial maintenance.

Divorce is not just the legitimization of the parting of two people. It also involves the fair assessment and division of their joint assets. Maintenance no longer depends on guilt or innocence, but on an attempt to assess the needs and previous contributions of the parties. In the Matrimonial and Family Proceedings Act, 1984, the emphasis was changed from attempting to retain the same financial position for both parties that would have existed if the marriage had not broken down to establishing self-sufficiency for them independently. Given that two can live more cheaply together than separately, this is a more realistic though scarcely easy aim. Arguments over maintenance and childcare arrangements take more court time and cost more in terms of Legal Aid than the actual dissolution of the marriage. This forms the background to ideas mooted by the Lord Chancellor in 1993 following the Law Commission's discussion as to whether further reform – incorporating a one-year moratorium before divorce during which such issues should be dealt with in a conciliatory manner – is appropriate for reducing both cost and conflict. Divorce has ramifications in other areas of law too, and proposals for the rights of a divorced wife to a share in her ex-husband's pension are before Parliament as I write.[33]

Most recent developments in the Church

Putting Asunder was a Church report contributing to the national debate. In 1971 a Commission chaired by Howard Root, whose report was published just after the 1969 Divorce Reform Act came into practice, affirmed the Anglican Church's own beliefs and practices, asserted the value of marriage as a rewarding relationship which ought to be lifelong, and discussed the revision of the marriage service.[34] It also made tentative proposals for remarriage if a consensus for such a course of action was found and the bishops believed it theologically acceptable. Over the next ten years the matter was debated and a further report prepared.[35] The General Synod of July 1981 then resolved that it 'a) Believes that marriage should always be undertaken as a lifelong commitment,' and also 'b) Considers that there are circumstances in which a divorced person may be married in church during the lifetime of a former partner.[36] During this period a new marriage rite was also written which attempted to show some of the joy in celebrating marriage, found lacking by the Root Report in previous rites. (See the *Alternative Service Book*, pp. 287ff.) The abortive 1928 rite was also officially allowed. The bishops also commended a service of *Dedication after a Civil Marriage* in 1985.

When an attempt was made to draw up a practical mechanism to regulate the remarriage of divorcees the proposals foundered on the rock of impracticality (see 'Pastoral Considerations', p. 169). The matter was left unresolved after 1984, apart from diocesan guidelines or rulings. After such an arduous attempt to cater for the conflicting beliefs of different parties within the church had failed, despite the wide range of options offered, there was little hope of a new resolution to the problem. However the actual number of remarriages in Anglican churches has increased fivefold since then. In November 1994 a motion was carried in the General Synod, with considerable support, which invited the bishops to 'consider the present practice of marriage in church after divorce, and to report'. Remarks by some of the bishops in the debate indicate that concern for the children of divorce, and perhaps an unwillingness to be pressured by those who have little use for the Church except for marriages, may influence their proposals.[37]

Also during the past decade the Synod resolved to accept as priests people who were divorced or were married to divorcees.[38] Despite assurances from the archbishops that their colleagues would not accept such candidates lightly, Parliament, whose approval is necessary in such matters, turned down the measure in a thinly attended late-night sitting which only its opponents had bothered to attend. Many in Parliament seemed indifferent, though some felt the symbolic role of the clergy as upholders of public morals. It is on points like this that the established status of the Anglican Church is tried. The matter was subsequently laid before Parliament again, given more serious attention by its Members, and accepted.

Notes

1. B. Rawson, ed. 'The Roman Family' in *The Family in Ancient Rome* (London: Croom Helm, 1986).
2. Hippolytus, *Apostolic Tradition* xvi. 23, Dix and Chadwick, eds. (London: SPCK, 1968). The editors suggest that this may have been the practice of the Roman Church before the ex-slave Callixtus lent the Church's moral weight to the permanence of slave women's 'marriages' and the security they should be given. He thus combined Christian standards of marriage with the belief that 'in Christ there is neither male nor female, bond nor free'. Whatever the law said about differing rights for men and women, the Church's standards should apply to each equally.
3. Kajanto, cited in Rawson, *op. cit.* Alan MacFarlane, *Marriage and Love in England, 1300–1840* (Oxford: Blackwell, 1986), pp. 218ff., discusses serial polygamy, pointing out the rarity of monogamy as a norm in human cultures. 'Christianity,' he claims, 'revolutionized European legislation with respect to divorce', and so transformed monogamy from meaning 'one wife at a time' to meaning 'only one wife or husband ever', unless death breaks the bond. Older scholars see it as the dominant mode of marriage. Cf. *Encyclopaedia Britannica* 1950 ed., vol. 14, p. 950.
4. Cf. Rawson, *op. cit.*, p. 26.
5. Clement of Alexandria, *On Marriage* (*Stromateis* III), Oulton and Chadwick, eds. (London: SCM Press, 1954), Introduction.
6. *Ibid.*
7. Within the Greek Orthodox tradition, however, there have been those who take the concession that 'it is better to marry than burn', found in Origen and other Greek Fathers, as allowing not only remarriage after bereavement but also after divorce, and so recognize divorce according to the civil law code of Justinian and subsequent legislators in Greece or elsewhere. Cf. D. Atkinson, *To Have and to Hold*

(London: Collins, 1979,) p. 43.
8. *Stromateis op. cit.*, III, 9:66.2.
9. Perhaps previous generations of Anglicans were aware of it. One Rector of Northenden in the 1950s, seems to have discouraged at least one couple from marrying on the grounds that the husband was a widower. They simply went to the nearby Methodist church instead. They felt the hurt ever after. MacFarlane, *op. cit.*, pp. 232 ff., suggests that there was a strand of feeling even in post-Reformation England which frowned on remarriage after bereavement.
10. Tertullian, *Ad Uxoren*, 1.5.ff. This was written when he was within the Catholic Church. He later joined the schismatic Montanists, and his later writings on marriage are somewhat vitriolic. We do not have his wife's reply. He is also critical of 'clandestine' marriages taking place among Christians without the blessing of bishop and community. He regards them as spiritually incomplete. *Ad Uxorem*, II.8., 9; *De Pudicitia*, 4.
11. MacFarlane, *op. cit.*, p. 223, referring to anthropologists and historians of comparative law. The later date is given by L. Stone, *The Family, Sex and Marriage in England, 1540–1800* (London: Pelican, 1979), p. 30.
12. For fuller details see L. Stone, *The Road to Divorce* (Oxford: Oxford University Press), 1990, p. 53f., and MacFarlane *op. cit.*, pp. 224f. These two scholars take differing views on the stability of mediaeval marriages. Stone claims it was neither a separating nor divorcing society, while MacFarlane characterizes marriage as 'very insecure'. Stone stresses the economic and affinial purpose of marriage before the seventeenth century, while MacFarlane is eager to see companionate marriage as an English pattern of relationship as far back as the Middle Ages.
13. I cannot help wondering whether it was the theorists and politicians who stressed the binding nature of the soldier's oath, at a time when Roman military power was in tatters. Barbarian mercenaries were not always as reliable as the

paymasters would have wished. Augustine saw the other 'goods' of marriage as applicable naturally, in non-Christian unions. However the *sacramentum* – the permanent bond – was, in his view, a peculiar Christian 'good' in marriage, not to be found outside the 'city of God' (*De Bono Conjugale I*. xxiv).

14. A. R. Winnett, *The Church and Divorce* (London: Mowbrays, 1968), chapter 1.
15. Martin Bucer's work was translated, with approval by John Milton, the poet and Clerk to Parliament, in 1644.
16. Additional information from *Encyclopaedia Britannica* (1950 ed.), vol. 7, pp. 456 col. 1.
17. Joan Perkin, *Women and Marriage in Nineteenth-Century England* (London: Routledge, 1989), p. 22. Her book gives a feminine, if not a feminist, angle on nineteenth-century social history and on women's efforts to gain equal status.
18. An elderly parishioner of mine, in 1994, recalled her grandmother speaking of a couple being 'married but not parsoned'. The term is not found in the *Oxford English Dictionary* though 'parsonified' is, with a similar meaning of 'married in church'. The grandmother would have learned it in the 1850s, which carries it back beyond a time when Register Office weddings would be common in the rural area where she lived.
19. *The Family, Sex and Marriage in England, 1540–1800, op. cit.*, p. 35. Cf. all of his Chapter 2. In Stone's later book, *The Road to Divorce, op. cit.*, he takes the view that divorce and separation were not part of the culture of late mediaeval England, despite this evidence from Norwich.
20. 'A Roving Round the County of Tyrone', (traditional, anonymous). In the song, the girl seems to have fallen for the blarney and then been deserted.
21. Collected in Ken Stubbs, *The Life of a Man* (London: EFDS, 1970).
22. Thomas Hardy describes a wife-sale in *The Mayor of Casterbridge*, but the force of the incident is that it is

irregular, even by the standards of such events. See also Roderick Phillips, *Putting Asunders* (Cambridge: Cambridge University Press, 1988), pp. 294, 334f. *The Road to Divorce*, *op. cit.*, pp. 53ff., doubts the frequency of such irregular marriages since they do not feature as grounds for prosecution in archdiaconal visitation returns in the sixteenth and seventeenth centuries. Perhaps they only survived in regions where neither archdeacon ventured nor landlord cared, or because the churchwardens who compiled the returns were not bothered by the conduct of those who had no property to pass on. In *The Family, Sex and Marriage in England, 1540–1800*, *op. cit.*, Stone describes a wife-sale at London's Smithfield Market, however.

23. Brushes seem to have symbolic value at weddings. Is it a symbol of domestic obedience or male prowess? I have noted besoms and yard-brushes among the decoration of French rural wedding cars in the 1990s.

24. *Seventeen Short Treatises*, Library of the Fathers (Oxford: Oxford University Press, 1847), p. 274.

25. Perkin, *op. cit.*, pp. 301–11.

26. *The Road to Divorce*, *op. cit.*, p. 408f. The duration of marriage may be the same but the psychological effects of termination by divorce are perhaps not. Quaintly, Stone speaks of the 1980 marriages in the past tense, though writing less than ten years into the period.

27. Figures collated from Perkin, *op. cit.*, Winnett, *op. cit.*, and *Encyclopaedia Britannica* (1950 ed.), vol. 7, p. 457 col. 2.

28. *The Road to Divorce*, *op. cit.*, pp. 50ff.

29. Perkin, *op. cit.*, p. 26.

30. *An Honourable Estate* (London: Church House Publishing, 1988), para. 70, p. 23. I take issue with their suggestion that changes in the Poor Law in 1834 introduced affiliation orders. Poor Law records for the Parish of Northenden include affiliation orders from 1823. Perkin, *op. cit.*, p. 158, also suggests the opposite – that until 1834 some women might prefer not to marry but to obtain an affiliation order

as a source of *independent* income, which they would have lost by marrying their child's father.
31. I am indebted to Winnett's account, *op. cit.*, for a great deal of this historical summary, though I have interwoven his information with material from *An Honourable Estate*, *op. cit.*, and from Stone, *op. cit.*, and from my own observations, correlations and conclusions.
32. R. Mortimer et al., *Putting Asunder* (London: SPCK, 1966).
33. The Trust status of a Pension Fund complicates this, and it appears that capital will not be alienated to the non-contributing spouse, but a share of the pension will be transferred once the beneficiary starts to draw the pension. This is less than campaigners for reform in this area want. It could also sow seeds of conflict, twenty or more years after the divorce!
34. Howard Root et al., *Marriage, Divorce and the Church* (London: SPCK, 1971). A further report, in 1988, *An Honourable Estate*, *op. cit.*, looked again at doctrine, legal theory and practice in the light of the growing prevalence of cohabitation, and of calls for revision of the Church's role in taking marriages.
35. *Marriage and the Church's Task* (London: Church Information Office, 1978).
36. Resolution quoted in *Marriage and the Standing Committee's Task* (London: Church Information Office, 1983), p. 1.
37. See *General Synod Digest*, no. 28 (Beccles, 1995).
38. While not wishing to condone sinful behaviour, the bishops were aware of many 'hard cases' in which, say, an ordinand developed a close attachment to a woman only to discover, as the relationship moved towards marriage, that she had been briefly married years earlier. I myself trained alongside a man who was called to the ministry in the 1940s, but had married a divorcee and was only finally accepted for ordination after her first husband died in the late 1960s.

SIX

Who Gets Hurt?

'Of course there's always divorce.' I had not been listening to the conversation properly as I signed the last of the marriage registers, so that I do not know what heinous crime her husband of ten minutes had committed – perhaps he had trodden on her dress – but it was a disturbing remark to overhear in the vestry during the actual wedding formalities.

'I didn't hear that,' I said pointedly, grinning at the same time. It was not a remark to let go, but neither could I make too much of it. If it appeared to be serious it could be held to void the marriage (at least in the terms of Roman canon law) on the grounds of lack of understanding of the permanent intention in marriage, or lack of that intention if it was understood. If, however, I played it up too much, they might remember it too well and feel their marriage was jinxed, or that it was a slip of the tongue betraying her inner reservations. 'Many a true word is spoken in jest', goes the English proverb, while the Bible shames our flippancy with what it says about the power and efficacy of words once spoken.

The trouble is, she had probably heard that phrase many times before. Secretaries in a big Utility were gossiping about their boyfriends and their wedding plans; one remarked, 'If it doesn't work out, we can always get a divorce.' Their older supervisor, a Christian who had seen for herself the troubles of a divorce, winced and could only say, 'It's not that easy.' She probably read about the possibility many times. 'Divorce rates rise' or 'Marriage rate at all-time low' are easier headlines from which to decry declining morals than 'Marriage rate second highest in Europe'. All are true. Perhaps because divorce is newer than marriage; perhaps because it is the focus of problems that the statisticians are asked to monitor, we write that the divorce rate per annum is 13.2 per thousand existing marriages, rather than that the 'staying-married' rate is 98.7 per cent.

She may have known friends or family who had divorced, and it hadn't looked too bad from a distance.

Is it too dramatic to say that she was already a victim of divorce, which threatened her own marriage at its very start? In a very general sense she was, in that any divorce adds its threat to the image of marriage as permanent. Should we say, 'Send not to ask for whom the bell tolls, it tolls for thee; Anyone's divorce diminishes me!'?

That is not in itself an argument to reduce or even ban divorce, since the good in a divorce procedure is that it regulates desertion and exploitation and provides a safety valve without which marriage would be diminished. Divorce is a way of saying that walking away is not easy, and that there are ways of making people live up to their commitments. Marriage may seem at times to be a gamble, but its debts are enforceable. This is a bleak scenario, with no ideal solution. Perhaps the most I can hope for from those who read this is not the thought: 'I have suffered this, poor me,' or even 'So I'm not alone', but 'I have caused this sort of hurt, forgive me', or perhaps 'I am causing this hurt, I will try to reverse it.'

Love's wounds

It is primarily individuals who are hurt. While the divorce itself may be a happy release, what lies behind it? A local woman hit the headlines recently by hanging a twelve-foot banner from her windows to announce that her divorce was through. What hurts had led her to it? and what scars will remain after the euphoria dies down? A divorce may mean safety after physical abuse, or peace after mental distress from a husband who is always criticizing and demeaning or a wife who taunts, but in the process of a breakup there has usually been a loss of self-esteem. The emotional investment of marriage has turned bankrupt; the trust has proved false, and the ability to make sound decisions has been found wanting. The decision to divorce may itself be a re-affirmation of one's self: 'I am me, and will not be used any more', but even that is an admission of error in the past. If that is not enough to create a poor opinion of one's self, such an opinion may have been reinforced by the repeated remarks of the ex-spouse, which are not exorcised by the divorce. Perhaps they have been repeated during the proceedings, and they ring in the mind even after they have ceased to ring in the ears.

'She drove me to it' a husband may say as he leaves his wife to live in bedsit-land with a girl half his age. That may be true to the extent that he found his wife's behaviour or attitudes difficult. It is also an attempt at self-justification when he has broken the promises of duty that he made to her. He suffers morally, if only by cloaking his sin in a denial of his moral autonomy. His ego is boosted and his appetite slaked, his self is gratified. The judge who tries his divorce may think him an utter scoundrel as he reads the affidavits, but then he meets the wife in court. To her difficult character is added the twist of self-righteous anger, enflamed by the insult to her womanhood. 'Hell knows no fury like a woman scorned' as she denounces his balding immaturity in the letter columns of the national newspapers (name and address supplied). It is easy to sound patronizing, but she *hurts*. And his lover? How faithful will he be to her when he tires of her?, and she to him when she has made her next career move? What scars will she leave with him?, and what disdain for men will she carry from him into the next relationship? Lurid fantasy? Some bestselling novel? No, thoughts prompted by a letter in *The Times*, provoked by kiss-and-tell journalism.

Behind many divorces there is pain and misunderstanding on both sides. Behind some there is plain sin, selfish opportunism, and lust for sex or power. But, as a counter to the words which began this chapter, 'There is always forgiveness.' It may sound glib, but an affair faced may be the point from which the marriage can be renegotiated.[1]

In another marriage, one party may be content and think all is well while the other feels frustration or restriction. When that partner leaves, the contentment is shattered overnight. All the shock of a sudden bereavement is made worse by the knowledge that this was not the inevitable hand of death but a personal choice by one who had been trusted intimately. Even when a couple's relationship has not been enriching for many years, the sudden self-justificatory announcement, 'I've decided to divorce you,' after years of frigid rectitude, can be devastating, as one spouse arranges to dispose of the other. Loneliness replaces company, and grief for the lost partnership plumbs the depths of depression. Again, self-confidence is shaken. At its worst this can be fatal. Two young men lie in Northenden churchyard. I buried them in the last three years. Both took their lives when they felt they had made a mess of their stormy marriages. Both were children of divorce themselves. A survey of mortality rates in West Sussex has shown that suicide is four times more frequent among the separated but not yet divorced than among the divorced, who are themselves twenty times more at risk than the married.[2]

While suicide may be the most dramatic evidence of the ill-effects of divorce, its effects are apparent over a wider field of health and well-being. No one can claim conclusively that this woman's failure to gain promotion through inefficiency at work or that man's contraction of cancer was actually caused by their divorces (and there may be an intermediate cause, such as an increase in a person's smoking). However in statistical terms, someone who is divorced is between 15 and 50 per cent more at risk from cancers than the population at large. Also, there are the financial consequences of splitting one household's resources two ways. It is impossible to catalogue all the deleterious effects of marital breakup on the couple themselves in a few short paragraphs. Nevertheless it would be wrong to give the impression that there are no instances where the relief offered by separation and divorce (from, say, violence or genuine mental cruelty) brings an improvement in well-being. But it is not just the couple who suffer.

What about the children?

A couple's most obvious fellow sufferers are their children. Again, separation may bring relief from violence, but what an outside observer sees as relief, the children themselves may regret as the loss of someone who belonged to them – however much they were abused. At a time in the children's lives when they might expect their parents' decisions to be made in their best interests they find the adults pursuing their own separate interests to the exclusion of the children's. They want their world to stay familiar, but the adults tell them that it all has to change – places, people, friends. Caught in a clash of emotions they do not know or understand the children are torn by rival loyalties and puzzled why their simple logic of being friends again cuts no ice. Worse still, they may be used as umpires during the disintegration of the marriage. Some adults seem to restrain their worst outbursts against each other until the children are present, knowing that their presence will prevent the outbursts going too far. The children's loyalties may be put to the test as after separation they are pumped for information about one parent by the other after a visit, or are used as go-betweens to convey messages that are too heavy for their tender years. They may resent this, but are also canny, and in time learn to use the power this gives them to work their own agenda. They may be used as weapons of the adults' warfare as their parents try to punish each other for the faults and offences which they see in each other's behaviour surrounding the breakup: 'She walked out on me, so I won't co-operate over contact arrangements.' Children may be loaded with responsibilities above their years as a lone parent turns to them for conversation and company or for support in emotional or practical ways which a spouse might normally give. Or it is assumed that they are 'too young to understand' as the parent shares adult confidences above their all-too-knowing heads. The scenarios are endless.

As like as not the children will have little idea that the break is coming. True, children can see through some of the things that adults try to hide from them. There is a story of parents who overheard their children squabbling, with the words, 'But you called me "darling" first!' Children may even pride themselves in seeing 'lack of communication' or some other buzz-phrase that they have heard at school. But for most children their parents' separation is a decision which is made without reference to them (even if the parent explains it as 'for the sake of the children'). Often they know nothing of the break until it actually comes. They are thus powerless, and those who should support their weakness are the ones who have caused it. Even if there has been some warning it may serve to confuse the picture more, since trial separation or a walk-out followed by return may give the impression that the real break is reversible. Perhaps that is the children's dream, even as adults. They fantasize about their parents reconciling at their own wedding, or project the reunion on to other significant people in their lives.[3] At the same time they may feel to blame. Was it their tantrums or costly presents that drove their parents apart? Very rarely does the blame lie here, but children can let it come to roost with them.

Those who care for the children – their parents particularly, but also grandparents, other friends, relatives or professionals – should be aware of these burdens and offer the children space and time to off-load them when they wish. Children should be reassured that the fault for the break does not lie with them. Their loyalties should not be strained either by the accusation that it was all the other parent's fault. With young children, the hurt may be buried deeper; with teenagers, it may come out as deliberate cussedness and worse. This is easy to say, but not easy to cope with.

Wallerstein notes the long-term anxiety about their own marital security among the children of divorce. At the same time, their moral ideals tend to be more rigid than their parents'. She also comments on their tendency to under-achieve as compared with their parents. British surveys show similar tendencies in education when the children of divorce are compared with a control group from intact families.[4] While no one can say that a particular individual's dropping out of college and subsequent bumming around, coupled with the dream of writing the definitive rock musical of the twenty-first century (despite failing exams in music), was caused by his parents' divorce before he went to school. However those who, like him, have come from a divorced family are perhaps twice as likely to have delinquent habits as those from intact families. To set that in context, however, more than 80 per cent of such youngsters do not have that kind of problem.

There also appear to be economic disadvantages that work against the children of divorce, though the chain of causation is more complex and difficult to prove than it appears. Are a greater proportion of divorcees' children unemployed because of their lack of confidence due to the divorce? Is it because the parent they lived with found herself in a lower economic bracket than she would have otherwise expected – as some commentators argue? Is the mechanism for finding a job among that section of the population where divorce is most frequent based on a network of informal contacts? If your dad knows a bloke who knows a man who is taking on workers, that is not much use to you if you have lost contact with your dad.

In the shorter term also, the children of divorce suffer as a move means disruption to their network of friends and loss of continuity at school. The loss of one of the most significant other people in their lives often causes emotional stress and behavioural problems, which in turn affect their academic achievement at school. They may well feel, in the immediate aftermath of separation, isolated from their fellow pupils and in a unique position, not realizing how many of their classmates are in the same situation.

The children of divorce often claim that they were not told what was happening and so felt even more powerless and bewildered. It is a fair criticism, particularly if the adults were talking about a split for some time. If, however, they were not talking, or were hoping themselves to work things out, or were uncertain until the last minute that they could dare to make the break, then the reticence is understandable and perhaps excusable. Why burden a child with what you hope may never happen? How do you face a child with what you cannot quite face yourself? How do you talk together to your children when you are unable to talk together yourselves, or have different tales to tell? The counsellors advise that it should be attempted, however, 'for the sake of the children'. Perhaps a trusted friend or godparent can act as an honest broker, sharing the grief. If, however, the break has been long-contemplated by one party but kept secret from the other, then the silence is understandable – and as reprehensible as the manner of desertion itself.

The sins of the fathers . . .

A further hurt for the children of divorce is that the incidence of instability in their own marriages is greater than that of the general population. This may be due to a poorer example of dispute resolution from which to learn; it may be that their anxiety for success is greater and their tolerance of stress lower; it may be that they are more ready to see divorce as a way out of difficulties. Perhaps additional health problems create greater stresses. Perhaps they rushed into marriage as a means of finding an emotionally rewarding relationship which they lacked from one or both parents, only to find their choice faulty and themselves insufficiently mature to sustain the relationship. Loss of contact with one parent, while the other is perhaps jaundiced against the opposite sex, and distance from the grandparents on that side of the family, may leave them with fewer people to turn to for advice and support in any attempt to maintain their own marriage. Thus the sins are visited down the generations as their own children lose out too. But the sociological observation in the second commandment is balanced by a promise that God's love can restore the thousands who do love him. Christian children of divorce have themselves supported this by saying how even though hurts surfaced many years afterwards, they were able to overcome them.

The older generation hurt too

Few parents can be happy if their children, even as adults, are hurt. If their children behave badly they may well take it as a slur on their own character or parental abilities. To see one's children divorce may be just such a hurt or slur. The mourning is felt deep down yet suppressed as they try to support the son or daughter who has returned to the nest. Their sadness is not seen by friends and neighbours since no stately car draws up to take the bride's parents to the obsequies. Their efforts have been invested in their children's good, but there is no dividend, and contact with the grandchildren may be lost. Their own sense of duty and the efforts which kept them together in times of strain receive a vote of no confidence, it seems, from their own flesh and blood.

Does that paint the canvas too heavily? When the 1947 diocesan conference of Chelmsford voted to exclude divorcees from communion (see page 109f.) were they voting, in their heart of hearts, not *against* divorcees but *in favour* of their own children's marriages? How much do similar hopes and fears influence more recent Church voting on divorce and remarriage? Such emotions are quite proper, for in any couple's marriage there will be times of strain, and effort and sacrifice need to be put into getting things right again. When a marriage has been a special struggle, perhaps because of illness, lack of work, the death of a child or some other difficulty, this is especially true – the silver, ruby or gold of the anniversary celebrations are well-earned medals to be worn with pride. Anyone's divorce, the divorce of a son or daughter, the greater ease of divorce in general, or the Church's acquiescence to remarriage after divorce can seem like stamping those medals in the dust. 'Was all that effort worth it, if it comes to this?' 'Why did we bother?' 'They walk away so easily today!' – or so it seems.

My heart sinks when I see a solicitor's letterhead as I open the post.

> Dear Sir,
> We are acting for Mrs Jane Suchabody in her petition for divorce against her husband Mr John Suchabody, and we should be grateful if you would furnish us with a copy of their Marriage Certificate. The wedding took place in the spring of 1985 or 1986, but Mrs Suchabody is not sure of the precise date . . .

I have actually received a request dated like that, so poor an impression did that marriage make. It is saddening to hear of such marital breakdowns, and to know there are others where the certificate has not been lost or torn up in anger so that I am not asked for a duplicate. Could I have said anything more, as I prepared them for marriage, which would have spared them this trouble or made them feel they could bring their problems either to me or to the vicar where they lived? I suspect not, but the question is still there. With the marriage certificate I usually include an offer to the solicitor of counselling if the couple will take it, and they figure in my prayers.

Anglican clergy were criticized early in 1994 for spending less time and effort on their marriage preparation than free or house church leaders. However it is a question of scale. I have about twenty-five weddings in a year, most of them for non-church-going couples. That is a splendid opportunity which the established role of the Church of England offers and which is lacking for those who only take the weddings of existing church members. There may be three sessions with each couple taking initial information, talking through the details of the service and the meaning of marriage, and then rehearsing the service. That is seventy-five sessions – between one and two evenings a week, yet despite all this it is little enough to counterbalance all the other influences in the couples' lives; little enough to gainsay the hundred years of propaganda which says that the Church does not want to know about divorce should it threaten.

The things people say

I have criticized the attempts made by church leaders to defend marriage by denouncing divorce and penalizing divorcees. That may seem unfair, but such attempts have created a climate of opinion which can further hurt the divorced. Many people have told me, as I prepared this book, of their own negative experiences. A staunch church member will speak of the hurt felt as a result of remarks and comments by other Christians. A less confident person might well have dropped out of church life. Some of those remarks may have come from people who were frightened by the threat of divorce and did not know how to cope or what to say. One finds the same situation following bereavement, when friends cross the road to avoid the widow rather than risk making her cry. Such behaviour hurts. Some of these attitudes come from a culture which is used to doing things by couples, sitting alternately around the dinner table – man/woman, man/woman. Such a culture subconsciously finds the newly single as unpredictable as a loose cannon. Another person will quietly admit to having gone through divorce years previously only after hearing a sermon in which it emerges that Abraham, the great father of faith, was a divorcee. Someone else, with few church connections, will speak of the cold reception divorced friends have received when making requests about their children's baptism. Others feel they need to ask special permission to be involved in the church because of a divorce, or are surprised that I am interested in the issue.

In the past I myself have contributed to the all-too-successful propaganda through over-zealous application of what then seemed to be the letter of scripture against divorce and remarriage. Yet I have come to believe the overall aim of scripture in this field is the prevention of hurt and injustice.

Chain reaction

When a second marriage takes place there is an opportunity for re-creation, healing and joy after the pain. Of course there is also scope for further heartache. One man's words, 'I'll never remarry; I'll never trust a woman again', probably speak for many people – women as well as men. Trust and self-confidence in one's sexuality, personality and value can be reborn, but it is not a rapid business. It demands honest examination of oneself (not easy when one's self-esteem has been demolished) and patient understanding and encouragement from a new partner. Old hurts can resurface – 'Stop nagging, will you! *She* used to say that.' – or may remain there, festering unidentified under the surface. Perhaps such an old hurt is brought up because an old habit, that underlay the original breakup, has not been acknowledged. Both parties need gentle honesty if this happens, yet it is likely to be at a time of stress or high emotion that such a reaction is triggered: lovemaking that is too violent or off-hand, disagreement that escalates beyond reason, an important event that becomes overwrought. It is not easy, nor for many people natural, to analyse the psychological triggers of their reactions and actions, though such triggers are not abnormal nor restricted to marriages. They are part of our normal human character. We train ourselves to contain or suppress their disruptive features most of the time, though for some people they represent a besetting sin. We may excuse such reactions by saying, 'I don't know what got into me then.' To recognize, face and maybe laugh together at the ghost may dispel it, but it is part of ourselves and may return from time to time, even when it has been named.

Memories and comparisons, especially happy memories, can be disquieting and may cause uncertainty for a new partner. This is perhaps most difficult to handle if reminders are constant because of joint responsibilities for children. Sharing the past may be an opportunity for healing and deeper knowledge of each other, or one partner may wish to seal off that time. If such sharing is merely an exercise in self-justification it has its dangers, and a new partner may become twisted by sharing hatred by proxy for the former spouse.

Step-parents and step-children can be sources of hurt to each other as well as sources of support and love. Hayman tells of one young step-mother sitting down with her stroppy new charge and reading such stories as *Snow White* and *Hansel and Gretel* until they both fell about laughing at wicked step-mothers,[5] but before the laughter there had been tears. Genuine love can face severe challenges: financial constraints, diaries controlled by which child needs to be with whom. Again, loyalties can clash and weaknesses surface. Will a father believe his children are teasing his new wife? Has he the strength to challenge them? What strange jealousies does his attachment to them rouse? What regrets do they rouse in him? When the children visit, does their parent switch from being a wife or husband into being 'autoparent', distant and detached from his or her spouse and from other reality, for some time even after they have gone?[6] After a visit, do the children take days or weeks to come down to earth, no longer hyped up by treats or concessions to awkward behaviour, or hopes of a return of the separated parent?

Healing love's hurts?

It is easier to catalogue the scars of a marriage breakup than to explain the rise in divorce, and easier to explain it than to remedy it. The observations of the 1956 Royal Commission have a contemporary ring about them.[7] The Commission noted the changed expectations of marriage, with men still expecting the traditional 'servant' role from their wives, who in turn were looking for greater partnership and companionship. They also noted a breakdown in the taboo against a wife's adultery resulting from the availability of reliable contraceptives, and the idealization of self-gratification and personal pleasure as against the historical ideals of reciprocal obligation and duty to dependants. They called for greater availability of counselling services, and the inculcation in the young of a sense of responsibility to the community. In response to a proposal that divorce by mutual consent be allowed, the majority view was that it would put too great a strain on the welfare services to whom would fall the necessity of maintaining the dismissed wife and children.

It is interesting to see Stone, as a historian rather than a moralist, blaming the rise in divorce since those prophetic words of the Royal Commission on the changing mental attitude to religion and the institution of marriage. He cites the cult of personal happiness, self-fulfilment and sexual pleasure, with its concomitant ideology of individualism and consumerism, and its stress on rights, not duties. Further, he points to the liberation of women and their widespread entrance into a labour market which appears to give them economic independence and offers far wider social contact with men. Finally, he notes in sociological terms how familiarity with divorce leads to its acceptance, which in turn allows its greater frequency thus reinforcing familiarity, and so on.

If this diagnosis is anywhere near correct, then to remedy the illness needs strong medicine indeed. While accepting these ideas, I would add a further refinement: that the greatest binding force in a marriage today is not social or familial pressures to hold it together, nor the stigma or financial disaster of its falling apart, but the affection which the couple feel for each other. What began as a supporting feature in the thirteenth century now must carry all the weight. Marriage is itself a great unknown. Two comparative strangers, with different habits and expectations grown in different family environments, commit themselves to live in close proximity for life. They each have a different family history, and echoes of it will be heard at unexpected times in reaction to unexpected promptings. The lifestyle and ethos that our culture has conditioned them for is take-it-or-leave-it, pick-'n'-mix, an economy that thrives on throw-away, built-in obsolescence. They are massaged by media which assume an attention span of less than thirty minutes. When such attitudes are applied to relationships with people, designed to last for more than thirty years, the strain shows. The long-term duty of married love cannot be spiced up into lively sound-bites of thirty seconds or eased by applying some 'special formula' lotion.

The healing of such a distorted approach to relationships begins long before marriage. It is not a matter of denouncing sexual immorality alone, or tilting at the windmill evils of consumerism, but recognizing how they infect our own thinking in every aspect (not just our purchasing habits). We need to name the demon to ourselves, and to those whom we may teach or meet, so that its power is tamed.[8] In thinking of our own marriages, and those of people to whom we speak or whom we prepare for marriage, we should highlight the duteous nature of love in marriage. That is not to say it is dour or grim, but that when a couple promise 'I will' in response to the question 'Will you love . . . ?' they are not just extrapolating their romantic euphoria into the next fifty years. Couples need to accept for themselves what society once provided for them: a sense of duty to each other and their dependants that carries affection through times of difficulty. 'I will' means 'I have chosen to work at this loving union.' They need to recognize that love passes through seasons. They will not always be living in the bright springtime of romance, but there can be a richness in the sharing of each season – even a winter of discontent – so long as it is approached with a readiness to face it together.

That is easy to write, but less easy to do. It means making time to be together, which may take some effort if shift-work or the demands of young children intervene. It means allowing time to be apart, for oneself or other friends (so long as that does not leave the other a 'golf widow' continually). It means sharing hopes and fears and giving each other time for that, recognizing each other's character. A wife may speak easily and quickly about her feelings; her husband may need time and space before opening up, even to his wife, or be silenced by her easy flow. One spouse may communicate better with actions than words, or by sharing an interest rather than sharing a confidence. (I learned this lesson early in my ministry from a group of widowers who articulated a deep friendship and mutual support through discussing and practising the technicalities of pigeon racing!) To the complaint, 'But he doesn't communicate,' I want to reply, 'Have you given him the space, and listened in his kind of way?' However it is also fair to ask him, 'Can you not learn her language too?'

Moving away from a couple's own remedies, many clergy would attempt to support couples with marriage difficulties, at least at a low level, though few are trained as marriage counsellors. However it is perhaps a case of fine ideals that falter at the individual level, for though there have been calls for the Church to put effort into this field, my local clergy in service training officer tells me that when he has put on courses to help with marriage preparation and support he gets few takers. There are also guidance and advice agencies such as Relate. The problem with these agencies is that they are overloaded and have a long waiting list after an initial appointment. When Leo Abse proposed the Divorce Reform Bill in 1969 he noted wryly that Legal Aid for divorce proceedings was then running at £4 million, but grant aid for marriage guidance was at £4,200. The figures have increased but the priorities appear the same nearly thirty years later. Thus, while it is right that this kind of reconciliation counselling should remain as a voluntary and charitable contribution to society, it needs to be funded adequately and securely if it is to carry the load that exists for it.

The same has to be said about any official conciliation service linked directly to divorce proceedings such as may arise from the Lord Chancellor's present Green Paper proposals. I was initially sceptical of what seemed like a move to cut court costs. However closer scrutiny reveals an honest attempt to build conciliation, with its possibilities for reconciliation and reduction of conflict, into the structure of the divorce process, a move which is a positive contribution to marital health. But without adequate funding and staffing as a long-term project such a move will be no more effective than Mr Abse's hopes that his Bill would lead to more stable families. The Treasury must accept that divorce conciliation services will be a long-term investment in stable marriage, and thus should not enforce a saving in the short term.

Right to remarry?

Clearly, so long as divorces take place, there will be those who will form new relationships, maybe live together and want to remarry. Christians may feel unhappy about this for themselves, though I have argued that the Bible's teaching does not absolutely disbar them. In addition, the historical context of the early Church drove its practice up a very narrow alley. However given the moral ambiguity of remarriage, should the Church actually perform such ceremonies or is it acting as Pander to what Jesus called adultery? For church members who conscientiously believe that God is guiding them this way, their church's support and counsel is important. But even if the church's boundaries could be drawn tightly and clearly, I do not think that such ministry should be confined to some register of members. There is an evangelistic message in the very fact of listening (whatever we say specifically about the Gospel to the couple). More than that, we can claim a right to contribute to their individual marital health, and to that of the community as a whole, by encouraging them realistically to face up to what went wrong in the past and to look at the Christian ideals of permanence, forgiving acceptance and mutual support towards maturity. We shall not succeed in every case, and we may get our hands dirty in the process, but we shall achieve nothing if our main aim is to keep our hands clean.

I remarked in the Introduction that it is easy to manufacture arguments to justify an action that we have already decided upon. The Root Commission saw that risk in a different light. Where there is a widely or predominantly held moral insight that a certain course of action is right, even if it departs from the accepted teaching of a Church, then it is the duty of theology to understand and articulate that insight. Even in 1971 the Commission felt that moral insight for change towards remarriage existed, and reasoned that it was not inconsistent with the New Testament witness nor with Orthodox or mainstream Protestant practice, nor even with the pragmatic reality of Western Catholicism – whose use of nullity belies the high theory of indissolubility. They asked the Church then to go beyond ecclesiology to the doctrine of God and his grace – 'a grace which can loose as well as bind, forgive as well as bless, create again ... and turn even the wrath of man to his praise'.[9]

Notes

1. See Peggy Vaughan, *The Monogamy Myth* (London: Thorsons, 1991), pp. 1, 2, 176ff. Despite my criticisms of her approach earlier in this book, she does offer positive hope of reconciliation and rebuilt marriages, not least in her own life.
2. J. Dominian et al., *Marital Breakdown and the Health of the Nation* (London: One Plus One, 1991), p. 22. Cf. p. 17. The percentages on cancer in the next paragraph are quoted from p. 21 of the same book, referring to several studies in the UK and overseas. Modern research should also try to bring the breakdown of long-term cohabitation into this picture.
3. This portrait of the children of divorce is inevitably sketchy. This paragraph and what follows is drawn from my own observations, and from J. Wallerstein and S. Blakeslee, whose work contains some of the most moving sociology I have read. *Second Chances* (London: Corgi, 1990), pp. 31–50.
4. *Marital Breakdown and the Health of the Nation*, op. cit., pp. 24f., referring among other things to long-term study of people born in a particular week in 1946.
5. Suzie Hayman, *Other People's Children* (London: Penguin, 1994), p. 29. There are clearly sad stories and success stories about step-parenthood, and Hayman's book is a mixture of hope and failure. Her basic recipe for success seems to be to anticipate problems before they arise, and to realize that parent–child relationships can be difficult, even without the complications of second parents and access arrangements.
6. The points in these paragraphs are prompted by Elizabeth Martyn, *2nd Time Around* (London: Optima, 1989), chapters 6 and 7; which confirm my observations from a far narrower cross-section of people.

7. Cited by L. Stone, *The Road to Divorce* (Oxford: Oxford University Press, 1990), pp. 402ff.
8. As long ago as 1970 John Taylor was suggesting that a Christian response to this culture should always be a humorous 'And who are you kidding?' *Enough is Enough* (London: SCM Press). Cf. my chapter in N. Sagovsky, ed., *Church and Society in the 1990s* (Nottingham: Grove Books, 1990), on the mind-altering character of modern society.
9. Howard Root et al., *Marriage, Divorce and the Church* (London: SPCK, 1971), paras. 141, 142; pp. 72f.

SEVEN

The Past and the Future – what is the good of divorce?

It was a picture-book wedding, with fine sunny weather and Amanda looking at her best. Tony was obviously very proud of her as he led her down the aisle to the strains of Mendelssohn's Wedding March. It can't have been much over a year later when I met her mother in the village. It came as a shock to hear that Amanda had come back home and that a divorce was pending. 'What went wrong?' I wondered. It transpired that Tony was violent, leaving Amanda bruised and shaken on a number of occasions. She had tried to sort it out and establish their marriage. In the end she had had enough and felt it was more than a temporary difficulty to overcome. I suggested that if Amanda wanted to talk, I should be willing to listen, but she did not take up the offer. The bruises were too deep.

I don't know the overall reasons for this breakdown. Had their relationship started out as one of those teenage sparring partnerships, which are expressed as much by ragging and manhandling as by gentleness and the sharing of ideas and interest? Was Tony less mature than he seemed as they stood at the chancel steps? Had he reverted to sparring after the warmer time of courtship when he found that their common interests were less than they had realized? Had he felt threatened by her closeness, or by her desire to talk and share emotionally more than he could cope with? Was it a pattern of behaviour that he had seen in his own family and failed to unlearn when he came to marry, even though he had resolved to avoid it? Was he saying, 'I don't know what gets into me', or 'Women!' and shaking his head? Had Amanda unconsciously 'asked for it' by not giving him space for his own interests or other friendships? Had she gone into the marriage thinking that she would sort him out, even though she knew he had a short fuse? Had he expected to carry on his bachelor visits to the pub as if nothing had happened on their wedding day to change his priorities or financial commitments? Was he exasperated by her overspending? Would more intensive marriage preparation have helped, or merely led them to go to another church or the Register Office (no questions asked) or to live together without the legal fall-back that marriage offers when something like this happens?

The functions of marriage

Marriage as an institution is not simply a private agreement between two individuals about their sexual and domestic arrangements, though twentieth-century Western individualism makes it seem so. The complex of family law which depends on marriage (or which falters where marriage is lacking) is in the background, unless some crisis develops. The marriage services barely touch upon this – they focus instead on the personal and emotional covenant of marriage – but where they do, they express it in a dated way. No longer is the woman transferred, property and all, from her father's authority to her husband's, even if the ceremony does involve her being 'given away'. Few dynastic alliances are forged at the altar, yet the couple still symbolize this by walking back down the aisle on their respective in-laws' sides of the church. Perhaps most relevant of all are the words in the ASB service in which the couple promise 'all that I have I share with you', for one of the functions of marriage is the establishment, transfer and regulation of a common fund of property within the present generation, or for bequest to children.[1] In marrying a couple are unknowingly gaining the benefits of legislation which regulates inheritance, for instance, in the case of intestate death. If they fail to make wills, the wife will still receive the bulk of her husband's estate, with provision for their children. Scope for family quarrels remains, but their legal outcome is governed in a way that seeks to be fair. The marriage makes it clear who is entitled to inherit and who is not. Only if the estate runs well into six figures does any of it revert to the Crown, whereas unmarried partners may find themselves bereft of more than a partner in such a case. Through recent legislation has removed most of the disabilities of illegitimacy, marriage is the most straightforward way of establishing parental responsibility and children's rights to inherit status and property from their parents.

Marriage still conveys an expectation that the couple will enjoy 'marital rights', despite recent court cases in which estranged husbands have been charged with raping their wives. It confers control of (or at least a very strong interest in) the sexual activity of the partners so that, quite apart from medical or emotional considerations, unfaithfulness can be taken to demonstrate the breakdown of the marriage.

In marriage the domestic and economic services of the spouses are shared. This may not be such a prominent function in British society as it is in cultures where a wife and children mean labour in the fields. Nevertheless, it is still true that 'two can live as cheaply as one' when it comes to buying or renting accommodation, sharing a car or performing basic household chores. (This remains true though roles within marriage have changed since the 1950s, when it was assumed that a typical wife was the home-maker and the husband the bread-winner.) This community of economy is recognized in the way in which Social Security payments are calculated (though to a lesser extent now in the assessment of tax). This may lead to a sense of injustice. Husband and wife can work and earn independently, and do not lose pay because of the other's employment. If one of them is out of work long enough to be dependent on social security benefits, the partner's income is set against the benefit claim.

A marriage ceremony is a rite of passage, legitimizing and defining the relationship between the spouses and moving them on from ties to their family of origin. They know where they stand and so does the wider society, whether that is their peer group or their tax inspector. They have an identity and moral responsibility in their own right, which is accepted by their family and friends and acknowledged in law. People who are married, even if they are below the age of majority, can for instance apply for a passport without it being countersigned by a parent.

The married state also includes within it an expectation of emotional comfort. This is, in its way, also a social function, though anthropologists do not register it as such. It is taught in the Church services, however, which talk about the 'mutual society, help and comfort that the one ought to have for the other'. It is expected to be *the* emotional support in communities where 'the family' means parents plus 1.8 children and where the mobility of that unit isolates the adults from their own parents, siblings or childhood friends. We may contrast the portrait of 'the captive wife',[2] isolated at home with young children while her husband works long hours, with the richer pattern of family and kinship which existed (and can still exist) in other communities.[3] Where this nuclear family is isolated, a marriage can be overloaded with emotional demands, having to provide not only the place where troubles and worries of the day are talked through but where intellectual stimulation, interest, variety and stability are sought. We are right to expect this support within a marriage; we are wrong to expect a marriage to bear the full load alone. Yet we also have to reckon with a society which sees sexual overtones in almost any relationship, so that it seems to threaten the unique sexual commitments of marriage. No doubt at times such fears are justified, but not always. This fear in turn places an extra load on marriage. We may contrast this load with Augustine's premise that supportive companionship was to be found outside marriage among friends of one's own sex.

Finally, marriage has a further function which is incidental to the regulation of the economic, sexual and hereditary activities of husband and wife and yet looms large in public discussion of 'the family'. It is a symbol of the well-being of society itself. The concern we show about widespread marriage breakup is not simply a (proper) awareness of the hurts it causes in the lives of individuals, or an acceptance of statistics relating family breakdown to crime, poor education or poverty. There is a threat to the community at large when its basic building-block, the husband and wife partnership, appears to be crumbling. The fact that people were saying this in 1900, when the divorce rate in England and Wales was less than a thousand a year, shows that this idea is not just a response to late twentieth-century social problems. We have already noted the significance of the hierarchical family unit of the seventeenth century as a source of stability. The recognition that the married couple form the basic unit of society is not new, of course. In the opening section of *On the Good of Marriage* Augustine highlights the importance of marriage as the foundation of society. However, such a symbolic function for marriage has dangers. If we subconsciously try to protect 'marriage' as a cypher for 'secure society' we must beware of sacrificing individuals caught in painful circumstances just to help Society feel good.

The functions of divorce

All this emphasizes the importance of marriage. Mutual legal obligations are involved which affect not only two individuals, but their children and the wider society. Emotional and symbolic factors also feature. At the simplest level, it would seem that divorce threatens the proper fulfilment of these obligations. Of course it is not that simple. Divorce is the end of a process, rather than its cause, and it begins a new process. Maybe the feeling that 'there's always divorce' as an easy option enables that process to begin, but to blame marital breakdowns on the availability of divorce is rather like blaming doctors for disease. The surge in divorces based on the fact of separation just after the 1969 Divorce Reform Act demonstrated how many marriages had already disintegrated.

To begin with the symbolic role of marriage, it can be argued that the Divorce Bill of 1857 preserved the institution of marriage as it was then known. Joan Perkin surveys the injustices felt by women in the mid-nineteenth century and the pressures for reform of women's property legislation as well as marriage law.[4] Those who campaigned for a change in women's legal status could actually complain that 'the Divorce Bill took the wind out of our sails', and had to wait another twenty-five years for something like proper equality in property rights. The 1857 Divorce Act simply gave women hold over what they acquired after separation, and so removed a key cause for disquiet. Perkin suggests that far from undermining marriage, and all that it meant as a symbol of propriety in Victorian England, the Act actually enabled conventional marriage to continue by allowing a safety valve when marriage's own inbuilt injustices were provoking disquiet and for other social reasons it was being questioned.[5] If the injustice of easy and male-dominated divorce was the reason behind the antipathy of Jesus and biblical writers towards divorce as it was in their day, then we should not lightly dismiss divorce itself when it serves to relieve injustice built into the structure of marriage. At the very least we have to recognize a positive function for divorce.

I doubt whether Amanda was very conscious of any symbolic role when she looked for relief from Tony's ill-treatment of her. Perhaps she felt let down by the institution which promises happiness ever after. Perhaps he felt resentment since she had not acquiesced to his expected role as a dominant husband. Perhaps in an earlier generation she would have explained her bruises as accidents or would simply have found another man, braving the community's ostracism but also unable (as the guilty party for deserting Tony for an adulterous relationship[6]) to seek a divorce she could not afford. Their relationship had broken down, and for them the institution with the mutual obligations it conferred had failed. If there were no mechanism for unravelling those obligations the institution itself would be side-stepped entirely, depriving the new household of any of the security that marriage is intended to bring. As the Lord Chancellor's Green Paper points out: '... many will simply leave the marriage and set up a second home and family outside marriage. This was a common occurrence, and a major cause for concern, before divorce law was reformed in 1969."[7] It is a moot point whether the reforms of 1969 have made such cohabitations by separated spouses any less common, or whether they have contributed to the rise in cohabitancy generally as people come to regard marriage itself and its permanence as less important. The Lord Chancellor's point remains valid, nevertheless. 'There must be mechanisms to enable people who are unhappily married' [I should prefer a stronger term since unhappiness may be temporary.] 'to reorganize their legal obligations when their marriage breaks down.' The old lawyers were right to use the term 'relief' when they spoke of a divorce being granted to an injured party. What Amanda sought was relief from Tony's ill-treatment, and a means of reordering her life and the finances of their house and other property. Had they been married longer there might also have been the question of arrangements for their children. In this case such instability discovered unexpectedly so soon after marriage might have warranted an annulment, but the fact that *she* found his behaviour unreasonable would be far easier to demonstrate than *his* mental disorder.

The good of divorce, then, is that it provides a mechanism for reordering one's life. In an ideal world it should not happen; everyone should live happily ever after. But we do not live in fairy tales and no human law can make a couple continue in love. As couples break up the law protects them and their children from injustice and adjusts their living arrangements and financial situation. Matrimonial law, and the related laws affecting children, have functions which match the functions of marriage outlined above.

A passage with no rites

The marriage ceremony is a rite of passage. Divorce is a reversal of that passage – as the 'brush divorce' demonstrated (see p. 100) but it is now largely without a rite. Even twenty years ago – when couples were required to attend court – the procedure was so matter-of-fact and routine that a judge might not look up during the two-minute hearing. One might expect a shout of 'Next please' rather than 'Petition granted'. That was before the 'special procedure' came to be applied in all undefended cases, so that neither party appears in a court now. Some may go out for a drink to celebrate or hang banners from their housetop, making an impromptu rite of their own. Others do not even know that their divorce has been granted until weeks later because their former spouse is not forwarding any post, even the decree absolute.

There are perhaps three points at issue here. The first is that the divorce legitimates and begins to define the new distanced relationship between the couple. There will probably be further legal business (at least under the laws pertaining in 1995) and personal jockeying to sort out finances and custody. This may be used to gain the hearing that the special procedure denied, for the second point is that the lack of a formal hearing can leave a sense of injustice. Accusations have been made (albeit to establish the fact that the marriage is irreparable, not anyone's guilt) which cry out for an answer even if no one wanted to prevent the divorce itself.[8] We are moral beings. 'No fault' divorce is convenient legally, but leaves people dissatisfied. Even if our morals do not stand the scrutiny, we want to justify ourselves. Perhaps only when we have tried to do this can we acknowledge our sins and seek forgiveness. If a marriage ceremony is somehow a stylized expression of joy and celebration of the couple's love, there may well be deep feelings that lack any expression at the time of the divorce. The marriage is dead but there is no funeral, and its ghost will not be laid. The lack of any formal hearing may save court costs and time, but for many people it leaves unfinished emotional business.

The 1966 report *Putting Asunder* presumed that a marriage would be deemed irretrievably broken only after a consideration of its circumstances – a proper hearing for both sides and the possible judgement that the couple could try harder, with support. This never became law since it would prove too great a load on the courts or their officers. The hope then was that such investigation might save marriages. Even where the marriage is not saved it has the pastoral value of reassuring the parties that they matter within the process which they initiated. Such a listening process would involve time and costs, of course, but the Lord Chancellor is right to revive the idea, and perhaps right in thinking it will save costs in the longer term.[9] In 1994, during General Synod debates on the subject of remarriage, it was suggested that there might be some liturgy for the dissolution of a marriage, not to override civil divorce but to prepare the way for a second marriage. Conscientious Christians might value some means of release from the vows of marriage or even the chance to make a formal confession of their part in a marriage breakup, but that is not what I am talking about here. It is the chance for couples to say, 'I am angry'. 'I did not do that', or even, 'Hang on, I am in the right', rather than confession. To be able to say such things in a controlled setting but where it will be heard by those to whom it is directed, is part of the process of grieving for the marriage and the re-establishment of self-esteem. It may not be the Church's ritual, but it should be someone's rite.

The third point concerns the procedures used to grant divorce. At present both the initial grant of divorce and questions of custody and property are handled by the courts, though the initial grant is largely a matter of a judge reading affidavits. Though it verges on the bureaucratic, and though the judges work with guidelines when it comes to assessing the financial settlement, it is still a legal procedure subject to argument about particular merits of the case. Only the matter of child maintenance has been transferred to a bureaucratic system. This personal element in the proceedings which is enshrined in its court setting is important. Marriage, with its attendant emotional implications, is too important and too personal a relationship to be disposed of as an administrative or even computerized process. Part of the impropriety of the Child Support Agency (CSA) is the transfer of such personal matters to an impersonal and implacable system, even if there is justice in the idea of responsible parenthood behind it.

Beginning the rest of your life

Divorce is the beginning of a new, distanced relationship. Except perhaps in the case of clean-break settlements between couples with no children, divorce is not the end. Even in such cases there may well be strong emotional links and memories, while wrangling over property and finance can take up to two years.[10] Where there are children, a shadow relationship goes on at least until they are of legal age: 'Whose weekend is it for the children?' 'Can we negotiate access for a holiday in term-time?' 'Why doesn't the CSA make allowance for the three nights a week they stay with me?' 'Will she have them ready?' 'Will he be on time so that I can get on with my arrangements?' 'I'm not going to let them spend time with her when *that* man is there!' 'Oh Mum, do I have to go and see him? I was going out.' 'Is she using me as a free baby-sitter while she goes off partying with her fancy man?' Even when the contact arrangements have lapsed there is still a ghost of the relationship: 'Will I hear from Daddy this birthday, do you think, Mum?' 'Will the CSA hassle me about his unpaid maintenance?' 'What if the children arrived on the doorstep and asked to live here?' The list goes on of possible points of friction, hope or fear. In some cases there is no intention to be awkward or to cause trouble, though the possibilities of misunderstanding and confusion are obvious. In other cases, where one or both feel aggrieved, there is scope for punishment of one by the other through non-co-operation or repeated recourse to the courts over the children. The effects may linger on. The recipient of a wartime 'Dear John' letter wonders whether he is acceptable in the church, to which he has returned after many years following the death of his second wife, and asks for a letter from the Bishop confirming his acceptability at communion. Children create an ongoing bond of their own, even into their own adulthood: 'I'd love to know what became of them. They're my only flesh and blood.'

There are of course couples who continue to work together constructively, either for the children or in other spheres of life, but who know they cannot live as husband and wife. There are also those who can neither live together nor entirely live apart. The marriages and divorces of Richard Burton and Elizabeth Taylor are a publicly known example. I have known divorced couples where one partner cared for the other in a final illness. There can be few such poignant sights at a funeral as the deceased's divorced wife crying in the back row.

Such examples are not common and some are in fact unhealthy. More frequent are the situation where the arrangements for the non-resident parent to keep in touch with his (it is usually his) children break down. As few as 57 per cent of children of lone parents (a high proportion of whom will be lone because of divorce) continue to have contact with their other parent.[11] Sometimes the motive may be deliberate self-denial (perhaps misplaced) in the knowledge that contact will provoke conflict that would entail the children being caught in the crossfire. Sometimes children are used as weapons in ongoing hostility between ex-husbands and wives. More often the problem is geographical as one or other partner moves away. Sometimes it is lack of interest and concern, sometimes obstruction. Whatever the reason the children probably feel it as desertion, or take it that they are to blame. Only perhaps 3,000 orders a year were made by the courts prior to 1991 denying access to one parent or another (out of over 80,000 cases). Since the coming of the Children Act of 1989 (operative from late 1991) different procedures apply and the equivalent figure (where the court must be consulted before a parent exercises some responsibility) is slightly lower.[12]

The common fund of property
Reordering of the fund of property established by the marriage is one of the prime purposes of divorce legislation. Children's inheritance is not affected, except that a new marriage may add

to the number of children who may inherit. At present this reordering may take several years. If either party is allowed to retain a house where the children may live or visit but which will need to be sold as part of financial redistribution, then the ultimate stage of the process may not be until the children are of an age to live independently. The fairest way to reorder this common fund has been assessed differently down the years. When divorce was a relief granted on the grounds of a marital offence, the guilty party might expect to lose out. Reform in 1969 removed this means of assessment and attempted to place both parties on the footing that would have existed if the divorce had not taken place. It became clear, however, that two cannot live separately as cheaply as they can together, and in 1984 the emphasis was changed so that both parties and the children would be given as firm a basis for the future as possible.

If John chapters 4 and 8 count for anything, as I suggested in chapter three above, we should work towards a justice and a pastoral concern in divorce and remarriage that is forward-looking and which supports those in a weak position in the social structure. Counting the monetary value of past contributions is as helpful to a renewal of life as is settling the cost of old scores. In a marriage the presence and emotional contribution of one partner may well have been the non-monetary factor that enabled the other to make larger contributions to the common purse. That, however, may be hard for people to accept in a culture which trains them to evaluate everything in monetary terms. They may feel unfairly treated and resent the other's presence in their life. Further complications are the way in which bargaining, say, for the speed of a settlement, can lead to the acceptance of less favourable terms[13] or the way changes in the general economic climate or other legislation can distort a settlement. Changes in the housing market may turn a burden into a bargain. Increasing longevity and the rise in the private pension market may make the wife's loss of rights to her ex-husband's pension of greater significance than in former generations (even if some capital adjustment was made at the time of their divorce to compensate for the loss – a matter under consideration in Parliament as I write).[14] Divorce legislation is the centre of a network of rights and duties. Pull one string and all are strained. The Child Support Agency, like similar agencies in Australia and elsewhere, transfers the assessment and collection of maintenance after divorce from the courts to an administrative organization. Given the poor rate of payment through the courts under the previous system, in which both the mothers and the fathers could rely on Social Security to meet the deficit, there was a good case for a more efficient agency to handle maintenance. However, I have already suggested that the personal justice of the courts (which weigh up individual circumstances) rather than the impersonal calculation by administrators (using standard questionnaires) is the right way for assessments to be made.

The most serious ethical question raised by the matter of the CSA is the balance of justice between the parties to the divorce. In a divorce, the standard of living of both parties is likely to fall. Wallerstein and Blakeslee noted this in their Californian sample, in which it was the mothers (with their resident children) who most lost out. This injustice parallels the British experience with a large proportion of divorced mothers reliant on state benefits and existing on a lower standard of living than their former husbands.[15] Thus it could be argued that the intention of giving both parties and their children a fair basis for their future had failed, so that in principle it is right to redress the balance by placing a heavier burden on fathers. Original settlements may have set low maintenance which has since been outstripped by inflation. It would be right to reconsider those arrangements. Catching those who made no maintenance payment at all is an equally just objective. However the ethical question is whether the balance of justice has been tipped too far in the opposite direction. There is a great deal of anecdotal evidence and little dispassionate study at present, since the CSA and the Government who established it have both the statistics and an interest in presenting their work as a success. I am told that in this parish there are at least half a dozen men who have dropped out of regular employment because the CSA assessment leaves them with barely anything for their own individual support. (And not all are committed to second families. This is for their own individual support.) Where is the justice if they and their former spouse and children are thrown back into the benefit system (or perhaps the black economy)? Where, for that matter, is the economic logic of it, since the exchequer loses their tax and National Insurance payments, but then pays out benefit? Who now supports the weak? In such a situation, where does weakness lie? New partners also resent being assessed for the former family's support.

The extended family

It is not only parents who have an interest and are willing to take some responsibility for the children of a broken marriage. Any child has potential ties and links with grandparents, cousins, aunts and uncles. Practical and emotional support may be found from them. Under present arrangements financial support for children and access to them by the non-resident parent is catered for, but contact with the wider family of the non-resident parent may be lost if the access arrangements break down or are minimal anyway. This deprives the child of much potential support and friendship, and the grandparents of their heritage. There is an emotional dimension in this, but perhaps a material one too. Grandparents may wish to pass on material or practical benefits to their grandchildren in ways that would be for the good of the children, even though their son or daughter cannot live with the children's other parent. I was pleased recently to hear of a family where the grandmother had kept some contact even though her son had withdrawn from taking up access arrangements to avoid the antagonism he felt they would cause. That is better than nothing.

Is divorce dysfunctional?

Divorce can serve a positive function in offering an ordered way of unravelling a troubled relationship like Tony and Amanda's and relieving her from a potentially dangerous situation. In an imperfect world marriages will fail. It is better that failure be regulated than that responsibilities be reneged upon. Regulation should protect the weak (physically, socially or economically) if it is to mirror biblical concerns about divorce. That kind of distributive justice will not necessarily focus on marital offences. The present English system attempts this, but justice is not always served. However, might there be a further function within the divorce system?

In practice, the divorce system functions to push couples asunder once they begin the process.[16] A parishioner found it difficult to persuade her solicitor that she did indeed really want a judicial separation because of her conscientious objection to divorce. ('No one bothers with those nowadays. They are only a stepping-stone to divorce.') And yet from 1961 to the present there seems to have been a decline of about 15 per cent in each year between petitions filed for divorce and decrees nisi granted, and a further 0.5 per cent before the decree absolute goes through. In some cases the overall cost or death may have prevented the case going further, but these figures indicate the possibility of reconciliation even at this point. Current legislation asks solicitors to draw their client's attention to the possibility of some form of mediation, but imposes no sanction if the solicitor ignores that requirement or if the client refuses it. The legislation is the last vestige of the proposal made in *Putting Asunder* that the degree to which a marriage had actually broken down should be investigated. Nevertheless, it seems that some individuals turn to their solicitor to ask about a divorce not because they are set on it, but as a means of shocking their partner into more appropriate behaviour or seeing whether their problems might be resolved.[17] Between 40 and 50 per cent of divorcees regret it, and 20 to 30 per cent hark back to their former spouse even after remarriage.[18] How far these findings reflect natural recollection and grief rather than a well-spring for reconciliation is unclear.

The Lord Chancellor's Green Paper draws on *Putting Asunder* and more recent studies to suggest again that opportunity for reconciliation should be built into a new system. Where such reconciliation proves impossible, the process should be so sufficiently conciliatory as to reduce the hurts and bitterness created in the parties and their children by a need to trade accusation and awkwardness. A great deal of comment about the Green Paper has suggested that its motivation is largely a Treasury-led desire to cut the costs of divorce litigation. While such concern is there, the predominant note is a desire to mend those marriages that can be mended for social and personal benefits; where that is not possible, to devise a way of unmaking them which facilitates just arrangements with as little added conflict as possible. It remains to be seen whether these ideas will work any better than those proposed by *Putting Asunder* when transposed into practical law.

The object of the Green Paper seems to be to create a structure which, among other things, upholds the Christian ideal of reconciliation. What is important is that resources are put into the conciliation and reconciliation services – both statutory and voluntary, secular or Church-based – to establish a comprehensive service and to enable this work to be done. If the Green Paper figures are valid[19] then approximately 185,000 petitions, at £550 each, will need revenue funding of £102 million per annum. The present legal costs of divorce are about £180 million per annum.[20] The Green Paper's figures are based on three sessions of mediation per couple. Figures from the Family Mediators Association in Manchester suggest that three sessions is a minimum, not an average, so that the Lord Chancellor may not see much change from the present £180 million after all.

Notes

1. I have discussed this at greater length in my *Cohabitation and Marriage* (London: Marshall Pickering, 1994), chapter 5, with reference to the anthropologists Edmund Leach and Kathleen Gough.

2. See the book of that title by Hannah Gavron (London: Pelican, 1968).
3. See the classic study, M. Young and P. Wilmot, *Family and Kinship in East London* (London: Pelican, 1962). Though now dated, this and the previous reference illustrate patterns of emotional and practical support (or the lack of it) which still pertain.
4. Joan Perkin, *Women and Marriage in Nineteenth-Century England* (London: Routledge, 1989), pp. 301ff.
5. *Ibid.*, p. 220. Awkward questions were being asked by social historians at the time about the origins of marriage, while others asked what kind of a relationship it really allowed between a man and a woman – cf. Susannah in Thomas Hardy's *Jude the Obscure*.
6. This scenario is based on a story told to me by a woman who visited my parish looking for her baptismal records. Her parents had not been able to marry because her father had a legal wife still living – drunken, but not adulterous – and he had no money to divorce her, nor any legal case since he was technically the guilty party. The registers omitted his name in disapproval, though he stood with her mother at the service acknowledging his responsibilities.
7. *Looking to the Future* (London: HMSO, 1993), para. 3.2, p. 13.
8. *Ibid.*, para. 5.15, p. 22, and the whole discussion in that chapter. The Lord Chancellor's point has been made to me personally by respondents after divorce cases. The way an accusation of unreasonable behaviour is made often seems more unreasonable than the alleged behaviour itself.
9. *Ibid.*, chapters 6, 7.
10. *Ibid.*, para. 2.6, p. 8.
11. Quoted in J. Dominian et al., *Marital Breakdown and the Health of the Nation* (London: One Plus One, 1991), p. 28, from a 1991 study by the Family Policy Studies Centre. J. Wallerstein and S. Blakeslee, *Second Chances* (London: Corgi, 1989), p. 38, also note a frequent loss of contact.

12. OPCS, *Marriage and Divorce Statistics 1993* (London: HMSO, 1994), p. 82. In some cases, of course, it will be the children who do not co-operate.
13. See *Looking to the Future*, op. cit., para. 5.22.
14. If the law is changed to extend pension rights beyond divorce, will pension companies still offer pensions payable to a policy-holder's spouse on the basis of his contribution?
15. *Looking to the Future*, op. cit., p. 24. See also para. 4.8; and J. Dominion et al., op. cit., p. 28.
16. A point made by John Bullimore, then a barrister practising in the divorce courts, in *Pushing Asunder* (Nottingham: Grove Books, 1981). The Green Paper is very critical of the way in which the adversarial system and widespread use of accusations of unreasonable behaviour in establishing the fact of marital breakdown actually reinforces the breakdown rather than enabling it to be repaired.
17. See *Looking to the Future*, op. cit., paras. 5.9, 5.10. Statistics derived from OPCS, *Social Trends 21* (London: HMSO, 1991), p. 40. Cf. *Cohabitation and Marriage*, op. cit., p. 121.
18. Andrew Cornes, *Divorce and Remarriage* (London: Hodder and Stoughton, 1994), p. 448, citing research done at Bristol University. The Bristol study is written up by Davis and Murch in *Grounds for Divorce* (Oxford: 1988). This reflects the wisdom of hindsight and the unforeseen losses of divorce, rather than a willingness at the time to work at reconciliation. Cf. *Divorce Today*, (London: One Plus One, n.d.), a factsheet, also quoting the Bristol study; it seems, as does para. 5.10 of the Green Paper, verbatim. But cf. Elizabeth Martyn, *2nd Time Around* (London: Optima, 1989), chapter 6.
19. The Green Paper figures are based on costs of mediation between couples who are paying themselves and have opted for such help voluntarily; that is, they are predisposed to make the best of the system, and not incur extra costs by dragging it out or punishing each other through it.

20. *Looking to the Future, op. cit.*, chapter 9. For the record, its figure of £1,565 compares favourably with the 'average' wedding cost of £7,699, taken from *Marriage Today* (London: One Plus One, n.d.), a factsheet citing a 1994 magazine survey. The likely proposals are for divorce on the grounds that after a one-year period of conciliation, which includes facing the financial and personal implications of divorce, no reconciliation has been achieved. This would lengthen the average time for a divorce to be processed and force couples to face the consequences of their split before it was irreversible.

EIGHT

Pastoral Considerations

The principles behind the teaching about divorce and remarriage in the Bible were not simply concern for keeping rules. If that were so, then Jesus' rigorous application of the Old Testament's mild limitations on divorce would not make sense. Instead he listened to the hurts people felt as a result of divorce and shaped his moral teaching to redress those hurts within the Law. Thus we see a concern for individuals who fell foul of the way the Law was applied. He was also concerned for the 'weightier matters' of the Law. One of these principles was the protection of those in a weak position because of the nature of society. The widow and orphan were typically 'weak' in Old Testament society. One of the reasons Jesus opposed divorce was that he saw how women could be exploited by it. When Paul applied Jesus' teaching in different circumstances in Corinth, the Christian virtues of forgiveness and reconciliation were high on his list of principles. Another was the importance of a saving relationship with Christ, so that a wife in a mixed marriage was asked to stick with it through difficulties so that her husband and children could see the Gospel in action. Where reconciliation and evangelism were no longer viable, Paul accepted that a person was freed from the obligation to let herself be hurt further. The urgency of Christian priorities should be taken seriously by committed Christians as they consider marriage – first or second time round – but they cannot expect that to weigh heavily in secular thinking, and if they believe that such priorities are better served for them within marriage they may marry. Thus a rigid concern for observing the letter of what Jesus or Paul said can open the way for social injustice or individual mistreatment under the guise of obedience to the biblical Law.

It may be that the principles of distributive justice, care, peace and the sharing of the Gospel might be better served by different courses of action than those developed in the patristic Church. The present aim of divorce law is to achieve as equitable an arrangement as possible for a couple's future, and future legal developments should make reconciliation more possible. Divorce may be the best course of action for a couple and in society it is a necessary provision. Nevertheless it is second-best. The 'first-best' course is the support of couples as they begin their relationship and even before then. People need to understand marriage as a deep commitment. Couples need to work at its permanence and richness, and when problems arise to attempt to reconcile their differences. That should be taken as read. But if we accept the fact of divorce in our imperfect world, what are some of the contemporary Christian responses to that fact?

The invisible people

'I don't see why we need to do that. We don't get any coming now.' We were actually discussing a ramp for the disabled (and mothers with pushchairs) to give access to a church set in a stepped churchyard six feet above the road. Perhaps the steps that those affected by divorce have to climb are less obvious, but there are barriers – some intangible, some explicit. These have led the divorced to be invisible in church until recently. The Church has been infected by the blindness of society. A school class can be half full of the children of divorce, yet none realizes that they are not alone. Christian women are assumed to have a husband somewhere, even if he does not come to church. Justice for the disabled may involve small, personal, practical steps to indicate that they are welcome. Similarly, the first step in giving a fair place to the divorced will be a small acknowledgement that they are among us.

Many churches have realized that simply to announce a 'Family Service' can make some people feel left out. What matters is not how it is understood by the *church family*, but by people who use non-liturgical English. They may be the single, the elderly widowed, or the family that does not contain two adults and 1.8 children. I have yet to hear a convincing alternative to the title – All-Age Worship comes nearest – but somehow the publicity needs to acknowledge that families now come in all shapes and sizes. It is not just publicity, however, that should take broken or reordered families into account. The content needs to match the message. For example, in churches where a family do readings and prayers, it should not just be the two-parent families who get asked. On Mothering Sunday or some other special day is the role of the mother alone or the mother with step-children fully recognized without being clumsily overplayed? To hear some prayers about Jesus in 'the holy family' one can almost see haloes hovering over the words. Yes, it was holy, but not because nothing ever went wrong. It nearly ended in divorce before it began (Matthew 1:19), and was so chaotic at times that the eldest son got lost (Luke 2:45), yet in it that eldest son learned his business (Hebrews 2: 10, 17–18).

When we pray, do we pray realistically about difficult marriages and irregular relationships, as well as saying nice things? The wedding service (ASB, p. 300) is happy to recognize the blessing and joys of the family life of all those attending, but unless a great deal is latent in the request for 'peace in our homes', those for whom joy is elusive are left without a prayer. The draft services in *Patterns for Worship* are marginally better. There are many items subheaded 'Family' and they include references to those at 'the end of their resources', 'hurt relationships' and the need 'to live sensitively within' a family.[1] Discretion is needed here, especially where biddings or extempore prayer are used, so that the topics for prayer do not become a source for gossip. In the wedding service, again, there is scope for positive preaching about patience, forgiveness and acceptance, for the benefit of all the guests – some of whom will be cohabiting or have experienced divorce. The introduction (paragraph 6 in the ASB) could be strengthened to bring out the healing purpose of marriage, whether first or second time around.

Wedding services are not the only situation where consideration of divorce is necessary. I noticed a woman creep into church one day, just before a funeral and sit near the back. After the service the chief mourner went over to her and brought her into the cortège. She and his father had been divorced for fifteen years but their stormy relationship still exercised a power over her and she wished to express her sense of loss. I had not known who she was as I took the service, though I knew of the divorce and had talked and prayed about what might have been – unknowingly giving her space within the liturgy to express her ambiguous feelings. Similarly, a baptism may be complicated by the absence of a parent as a family splits up, or because grandparents are remarried and all want to be there. The request for a child's baptism may be part of the sniping between parents, but unless that is so, I should be loath to apply to the child of divorce any different policy from what is used generally.[2] With many young parents present however, the baptism service is an appropriate setting to affirm the Christian lifestyle: of honour to parents, and restraint of the temptation to covet one's neighbour's wife – or husband.[3] The use of the Commandments should be mandatory in a baptism service.

A time to meet

One frequently hears the complaint among regular churchgoers that people have no sense of commitment and cannot be relied upon to turn up at services, events or activities. For those caught up in the aftermath of separation the reason may be practical rather than a matter of apathy. The statistics in Chapter 1 show how many people that may involve. Children may seem irregular attenders at a choir practice or cub group because it clashes with access arrangements. Single mothers, or maintenance-paying fathers, may need to work over and above the day job to cover their liabilities. Some churches are moving from 'Sunday'

Schools to midweek Bible clubs to meet this challenge. Given the leaders' commitments this is not always possible, but it is fair to ask whether poor attendance is due to this, rather than disinterest.

Contact itself can be a problem. A bedsit or the park on a wet Sunday afternoon are not ideal places to maintain a relationship between non-resident parent and children. The feelings between divorcing spouses can run so high that they are afraid to meet and hand over the children. For a while our curacy house was used by one couple as a dropping off and collecting point. Christopher Compston highlights the value of the loan of a house and garden for an afternoon by a friend.[4] Both situations are practical ways of supporting divorced or separated families.

There will be some church events and meetings that divorcees can get to, and such groups will be of importance to them. Unless these are very rigid teaching sessions, the problems of separation can be talked about and support and advice sought. So long as the same individual's same grievance is not dwelt upon at every meeting (in which case separate counselling is probably called for, with a request that the matter is not discussed in the group) this is surely one of the benefits of such groups. We all need the support of friends, especially when something touches us to the emotional core. In some areas, where single parents make up a large proportion of the population, churches have deliberately set up parent and toddler groups, perhaps with the aid of the Church Urban Fund, as a means of serving the community. While all parents are welcome, the purpose of the group is the support of the divorced or separated, most of whom will not have an overt church commitment. The next door parish may have a large membership of young professionals, and the mother and toddler group's ostensible function is Christian fellowship and Bible study, or discussion for those now at home with young children. On the sociological level it gives contact with other adults outside the home to those suddenly transformed from 'rising young executive' to 'someone else's mum'. That in itself is a support for their marriages, though it is a very different group from the previous one. If separation or an affair strikes, then the network of friends too can be a support, though there may also be a sense of shock – it shouldn't happen to us. Members of the group or an older, wiser church member may help to bring the couple back together again, or be there as moral support when those efforts fail. The same opportunity is there in mixed Bible study groups or a specialist men's group, so long as there is no tacit conspiracy that makes divorcees invisible.

These ordinary groups in a church are those which may have a role in supporting divorcees in the shock of the immediate separation or during the long haul of living with its consequences. Few churches are big enough, or are situated so much among the divorcing classes, as to be able to run special groups for those in this situation, but they are a possibility. Andrew Cornes describes the healing effect of the short-term group of a dozen or so divorcees convened in connection with the preparation of his book *Divorce and Remarriage*.[5] Given that he comes down strongly against remarriage for Christians after divorce, he is right to stress the importance both of continuing support for those who are single again from among the church fellowship and also of help to overcome the initial reactions. Christopher Compston describes seminars run twice a year over five-week periods at the church of which he is a member, led with clergy-backing, by lay people some of whom are themselves divorcees. Members of these seminars are then integrated in other fellowship groups.[6] This says something of the size of the church, its location and its effectiveness in sharing the Gospel among people in this deep emotional trouble.

Leaders and members of such groups, lay or ordained, will have opportunities to support people facing separation or its aftermath on an individual basis, and all members should accept an obligation not to turn confidences to gossip. My own experience, which reflects partly the nature of the churches where I have worked and my own character, has centred more on this kind of individual support. My discussion with couples planning their marriages also centres on meetings of the three of us, rather than a group discussion or video material such as is available.[7] Such support will involve personal interest when someone's self-esteem is undermined; listening to complaints about the legal system, the CSA or the ex-spouse; sharing the hurt of false accusations (perhaps even of child abuse) made in the heat of a battle for custody or access. I sometimes feel, however, that the clergy are the last to hear about an impending break in a marriage. It may be their reputation for always being 'so busy', or a feeling that they wouldn't know anything about marital problems anyway. I suspect, however, that it is partly the result of a hundred years of propaganda against divorce, such that those who have nerved themselves for so traumatic a step are afraid they will be told not to take it, and will be loaded with additional guilt rather than helped either towards reconciliation or through the trauma. It is right that they should be asked to think carefully. They almost certainly will have done, but an outsider's angle may be useful. In the end it is they who have to live with the decision, which should be respected.

In a booklet on integrating men in the church, Gavin Wakefield suggests (in his only reference to divorce) that if sexuality is discussed in a men's group the topic needs to be sensitively handled in case any divorcees are there.[8] That in itself is a give-away line. A colleague once described how on arrival in a new parish he was struck by the very low proportion of men in the congregation. As he got to know the church he discovered that a very high proportion of the women were divorced. They had remained in the locality when the break came and had stuck with the church, while their ex-husbands had moved out. When three other divorces happened in the church the husband remained in the church in only one case, and that was because his wife had made the break and moved away. The hundred years of propaganda, the sense of guilt over the divorce, the dislocation of moving out, and a feeling (rightly or wrongly) that the church has sided with the wife could all combine to sideline men more than women after a divorce. Conversely, my friend found that where he was able to offer support to men dealing with the aftermath of divorce, it was both appreciated and brought some involvement with the church, though not thoroughgoing membership.

Schools

With so many children affected by divorce, some brief remarks are appropriate about the way it is handled at school, particularly at church schools, where church-appointed governors will have considerable control over admissions, the appointment of staff and the general ethos of the school. Children affected by a divorce should be helped to see that they are not on their own; some of their class-mates may be in the same situation. Topic work on 'families' or self-introduction by way of family histories should enable them early in their school career to accept themselves and their fellow sufferers as sharing an all-too-common background. Teachers may be aware of the learning or behavioural difficulties that this can cause, but as true professionals will understand and will not let this lead to discrimination. It is probably appropriate to use the term for a step-parent which the children themselves use. If he is just 'John' to the child, the teacher should not be so pedantic as to insist on 'Uncle John' or 'Mr Smith'.

It is difficult to imagine any school deliberately penalizing the children of divorce in their admissions policy. Unconscious discrimination could take place, however, if a church school had a requirement, say, for regular attendance at church, yet access arrangements with the absent parent prevented frequent enough attendance, or if parents were required by the school to be communicant churchgoers yet were refused communion as remarried divorcees by their own parish. Even an argument put to an appeals panel that 'half our children already come from broken homes' could lead to the exclusion of further such applicants. If a concern for justice is central in the Bible's handling of divorce, church schools should write policies to cater for such situations. 'Justice' may be spoken of in grand pronouncements, but ultimately it is expressed in particulars.

Both within and outside its schools the Church has a teaching role, though to change moral attitudes it opposes far more persuasive forces than even the most dedicated teacher or preacher. It is easy, for instance, to get children to assent to the idea that they should not tease classmates or 'wind up' members of staff, but in the playground two hours later they will conspire to do so. RE and Personal and Social Education which enables young people to live communicatively with others contributes to good marriage relationships. What such teaching (or preaching) is up against, however, is a culture in which children perhaps from the age of four have a TV or stereo in their own bedroom and so do not need to learn how to communicate or negotiate even with other members of their family of birth, let alone with a comparative stranger in marriage. Christian moral education as applied to marriage and divorce should not just be a denunciation of sexual immorality, but an attempt to raise the awareness of adults and children of their duties and obligations to each other, as well as the rights of 'freedom' and 'choice' which they will catch from the advertisers.

And remarriage?

Assuming the general principle that remarriage is morally permissible in some circumstances, here are two further questions. A pastor may perhaps put them, but the answer has to lie with the individuals concerned. Firstly, 'Is remarriage right for *you, now?*' In other words, has the individual sorted out the problems which arose from the divorce, and also those which led to it, sufficiently to be able to cope with a new intimate relationship? And secondly, 'Is marriage with *this person* right for you?' Perhaps it is this relationship that has enabled the hurts of the previous one to be healed, so both questions are answered in one. Or perhaps they are two lonely people grasping for support. It is up to the pastor to help the couple answer those questions for themselves, and to build on the answers so that their marriage is as well-founded as possible for the future. Perhaps they are questions to be asked at first marriages, as well as second ones. The charity One Plus One is engaged in specific research into this last point, and is offering answers in greater detail than can be given in this book.⁹ As the Anglican Church looks again at remarriage, it should work towards a procedure based on forward-looking support and counselling, rather than assessment of whether it is right to let the couple marry in church.

Between 1981 and 1984 the General Synod put a great deal of time and effort into discussing ways of regulating the remarriage of divorcees in Anglican churches, after accepting that in some circumstances this might be permissible. They produced their published report, *Marriage and the Standing Committee's Task*, and draft resolutions and regulations for the clergy. In the end the sheer complexity of the procedures (with some principled opposition) grounded the whole project. They wished to avoid legalism, but the need for consistency led to a draft questionnaire occupying seventeen A4 pages. The procedure involved the clergy of the couple's parishes, then the Bishop of their diocese, then a team of regional assessors, and finally a decision made by the Bishop. Only those able to cope with bureaucracy would remarry in church! As a result, the situation reverted to what it had technically been before, namely the sole discretion of an incumbent as to whether he used his rights in English law to conduct the wedding. Some dioceses, however, recognized that expectations had been raised and asked clergy to pursue at least some of the inquiries suggested by the Standing Committee and to consult their bishops before conducting such a wedding. For instance, clergy might ask whether obligations to children were being met honestly, whether the divorced party had learned anything about himself as a result of his failed marriage, or whether there was any sign of Christian commitment from the couple.

Prior to these developments I received a number of requests to conduct second marriages which I turned down (apart from the 'nullity' case in Chapter 1). I took one 'Blessing' after a civil marriage, but found this an unsatisfactory resolution of the dilemma (as did the couple). If remarriage is a spiritual impossibility or breaches Christ's moral absolutes, then it is hardly logical to purport to offer prayers to sanctify a legal ceremony that is unholy *ex hypothesi*. Services of blessing are appropriate where a couple desire to bring a Christian dimension into their civil marriage at a later date. I was recently delighted to lead a thanksgiving service (written around the ASB marriage service) for a golden wedding celebration.

When a couple approach me to take a marriage which will be the second for one or both of them, I would always expect to meet with them face to face. It seems to me to be common courtesy, quite apart from Christian honesty, to hear their case and explain in person why I will or will not take their wedding. It is hardly fair to leave my wife (as like as not) to say over the phone, 'No, he doesn't do that sort of a wedding.' The Standing Committee were surely right to stress the pastoral need for people to feel that they had been listened to, even if turned down in the end.

Asking questions about the previous marriage or possible reconciliation, especially with a new partner sitting in on the conversation, is a delicate matter. One does not want to open old wounds, but some basic facts are needed. Also, both parties need to understand how the past can mar their present. Some idea of when the first marriage broke up is more informative than the date of the divorce decree. When a marriage splits many people are content to be away from their partner. Some will initially hope for reconciliation even if their partner is cohabiting with someone else or contact is totally lost. Only when they realize that there is no likelihood of reunion, or when another possible partner comes on the scene, are they ready to face the hassle and expense of legal proceedings. Thus it may turn out that the new relationship began before the old marriage had formally ended, but was not in itself the cause for that breakup.

Having said that, I would not be willing to take the marriage of a couple whose adultery together had been the cause of the split up of the first marriage. Where that has been the case perhaps couples self-select themselves away from a church wedding, but I may be naïve and too easily deceived about this.

Questions about the previous marriage might include: When did the previous marriage begin and end? What were its circumstances? What have you learned about yourself from what happened? What arrangements have been made for the children? There are two purposes in asking them. Firstly, sub-Christian ideas about the nature of marriage may come out. I try to encourage the couple to think things out for themselves by means of questions. More significantly, there may be scars created by the first marriage which will mar the new one: 'You're talking just like she did!' is not the recipe for a happy relationship. The scar may be caused by the ex-spouse, or maybe the attitude of the person asking for remarriage was the real problem. I usually ask what the former spouse would say was the reason for the separation. It is a difficult question to ask, and to answer, particularly with the future new spouse sitting in the same room. Answers range from the self-justificatory, 'She wouldn't, it was all her fault, she was the guilty party', through the non-committal, 'We just drifted apart', to the more self-critical and constructive, 'I never really communicated with her', or 'I was never there, I worked away a lot.' I am least happy with the first answer, since it seems unlikely that there were no mistakes on the one side and all were on the other. It indicates an unwillingness to examine oneself and attempt change where necessary, even if the error was merely over-hasty and over-youthful marriage in the first place. I sometimes quote Walter Trobisch, who writes of only remarrying guilty parties – in other words those who accept their share in the faults of the first marriage and will work at correcting them.[10]

The answers, however difficult, are ones the new spouse needs to hear. The couple probably have talked over what went wrong in the past and resolved to avoid such mistakes in the future, but if not I hope my questions prompt them to do so. Even if they have discussed the issues, they may feel unduly sure that it won't happen again, or not realize how a flashback may affect the present relationship as a raw nerve is touched. Similarly, financial obligations or the presence of step-children may cause tensions in the new marriage. I cannot tell them how they should negotiate round these potential problems, but I can encourage them to think about them. This is not a prerequisite of taking the marriage, but it is a piece of low-key marriage counselling in advance.

The Standing Committee suggested that a clergyman should instruct the couple in the Christian understanding of marriage as a lifelong commitment, and refer them to canon B30, asking them to sign their assent to it. This may be a way of stressing the seriousness of remarriage and the high value that Christianity places on lifelong marriage. It is, however, a very legalistic way of making a point. It is one thing for a teacher to state a series of facts, but whether his pupils have internalized those facts is a different matter. It would be easy for a couple to nod sagely as their vicar reads through canon B30 and then to sign on the dotted line – just another hoop to jump through to get their desired church wedding. I have usually found that one of the couple at least, perhaps the divorcee, will volunteer an affirmation that 'it is for keeps this time', or words to that effect. This may just be a hoop that they know I will expect them to jump through. Or they may know it is what I will want to hear, even if they have doubts about their ability to live up to it. More often it is a genuine statement. They know the pitfalls, they have had their fingers burned once, but they do mean it to last this time. I aim to reinforce that intention, and perhaps offer some help in achieving it. I make the point not by quoting canons but by joking with them about 'the next fifty years' as I talk over the serious promises of the wedding services. This may be a more effective way of enabling learning and instructing the couple.

I would hope to tell them at the first meeting whether I will take the service. Sometimes I need to consult the Bishop, and will point out that it is not a foregone conclusion that we will say yes. Wedding planning is such that they may already have booked a reception – as is the case with many first-timers, too. However that in itself is no reason to agree to take someone's wedding (though it is a reason for the courtesy of as quick a response as possible). Looking back at the General Synod proposals of 1984 it seems most unrealistic for them to have proposed asking a couple to wait for over six months while the assessment and consultation process took place before even beginning to make firm bookings. Not least among the complications in that procedure is the fact that a large proportion of divorcees who propose to marry are already living with their fiancées. When that is the case, quite apart from the question of remarriage in church and the morality of it, there are strong reasons for regularizing the relationship so that each has the legal security of marriage. Particularly if the couple say that they will not bother to marry if they can't have a 'proper' marriage in church, I point out the legal complications that exist for a cohabitant couple in the event of breakdown or tragedy and refer them to a lawyer.

If I feel able to take their wedding I normally ask to use a particular prayer, which I first wrote when the Synod discussions were taking place in 1984. It asks for God's forgiveness, and healing of the past and guidance for the future, without laying blame in any heavy-handed way. The purpose of this prayer is twofold: It is a genuine prayer that God will heal and remake this couple's lives. It is also a public recognition that there has been a divorce, for whatever reason, and that neither the couple nor the Church is pretending that it never happened or doesn't want to know. (See Appendix II.)

There are also legal requirements and practical considerations. I do not agree a date when I know I cannot take the service myself, since I can hardly impose my moral decision on a stand-in. There could be complications, especially if an ex-spouse may not co-operate in the normal access arrangements with the children on that day, or is feared to be unstable enough to cause a scene. Also, is it appropriate for the bride to be 'given away', in the traditional manner of first weddings, if she has been divorced? That may depend on how long her previous marriage lasted, and whether she went back home or remained independent. Moral support is needed. If and when there is an official acceptance of remarriage in churches, guidance in the rubrics on this matter might be helpful. It would give weight to a local minister's suggestion that a father might not be the right person to give away a bride who left home to marry or cohabit ten years ago, or who has teenage children (who may themselves be the appropriate moral support for her).

The Standing Committee proposed that second marriages be preceded by banns, coupled with a declaration that after due consideration the Church had granted dispensation from its normal practice. In the event, there is now no procedure for granting this. Banns are legally valid but some dioceses advised that a Superintendent Registrar's certificate is the more appropriate preliminary to such a wedding. Their reasoning was twofold: Civil Registrars are more used to handling divorcees and checking the validity of their papers. While I would want to see the divorce decree, if only to see what 'fact' the court thought relevant in granting it, I am not sure that I am competent to know the validity in England of a document purporting to be a decree nisi from New York. The Registrar will have access to the appropriate court to check any such uncertainties. The other reason, particularly relevant if the couple live in separate parishes, is that while I am prepared to look at each request on its merits, colleagues may be opposed in principle to remarriage and so object to reading banns for such a case. Their wishes command respect also. The Registrars need confirmation from Anglican ministers that they are prepared to recognize their certificate as valid for a particular wedding, since they are not bound under the Marriage Act of 1949 to accept it. They will also require confirmation that the parties are eligible to be married in a particular church, by virtue of residence or membership on the electoral roll. As things stand in 1995, the Archbishop's legal advisors state that Special Licences are not granted if one or both parties to a proposed marriage have a former partner still living, while it is not normal for ordinary licences to be granted in such circumstances either. So long as the Church's position is ambiguous such reticence shown by the bishops is understandable. The action of a lone clergyman creates less of a precedent.

The Standing Committee discussed the Eastern Orthodox provision of a separate, somewhat penitential form of service for second or third marriages after divorce, but did not favour such a service. They did propose that the declaration of the dispensation for the remarriage contrary to normal practice should be read as a preamble to the marriage service if it had not been used when banns were read. Otherwise the existing 'authorized services should be read without diminution, amendment or addition'. It is a legal requirement (quite apart from theological considerations) that the introduction, challenges and promises at the beginning of the service should not be altered. The prayers (especially in the ASB) are more variable, as are the readings, hymns and sermon.

The Standing Committee felt that formal penitence where the parties requested it, or informal discussion of guilt and forgiveness, belonged to the private preparation for the wedding rather than the formal liturgy. A prayer for forgiveness and grace for the future is allowed for in their guidelines,[11] but they stress that 'This is not a different sort of marriage.' Such a prayer within the actual service is the right approach, with the possibility that a hymn, chosen by the couple, might also express their wish to turn from past mistakes. A revision of the introductory section for *all* weddings, to affirm more strongly Christian teaching in the face of a world where cohabitation and divorce are increasingly prevalent, would be welcome however. Whether divorcees, or at least some divorcees in some circumstances, might be asked to make a public confession at another time prior to remarriage is a question which might open a way for the Church to deal with the scandal of remarriage after a notable divorce or among prominent church members. The sins that surround divorce should not be the only sins dealt with in such a way, however.[12]

One of the questions raised by the Standing Committee is whether the applicants are active church members or show signs of becoming such. There are several difficulties here. It is true that a request for any marriage in church, not only a second marriage, is an opportunity to speak of God's saving love both as a fact and as an appeal for our response to him. In looking at the introduction to the services, which speak of marriage representing the union between Christ and his Church, and at the central blessing, which expresses God's good will for the couple even before they turn in prayer for help to uphold their promises, I attempt to highlight God's reality and grace. In the light of St Paul's motives as he discussed staying together, divorce and remarriage, it is surely right to see this situation as one in which the Gospel can be shared. However I do not feel that I can imply, 'Unless you agree with me and I see you in church regularly, you can call off the wedding!' If the couple's encounter with Christianity and Christian worship is positive and attractive enough, then they will turn to Christ through the second marriage. But we are not in the business of making 'rice Christians', who belong to the church because of the favours we give them. It would also be inconsistent to set this as a prerequisite for those marrying a second time when we do not (and legally cannot, at present) make the same demands of first-timers. In any case, marriage is a gift of God in creation, part of his common grace to all humankind rather than a feature of his saving grace alone.

Does this approach work? Given that people often move away when they marry, it is difficult to tell. However I see as great a proportion of second-timers coming back to church from time to time as I do first-timers. For the same reason it is difficult to know how successful my own low-key marriage-counselling approach to remarriage has been. Roughly speaking, it seems that I have received more reports of something going wrong with first-time marriages than from those who remarried. This approach is simply one person's experience and practice of trying to make remarriage a useful pastoral and evangelistic ministry.

And what about clergy?

Given the public role of clergy families and the accessibility of their homes to all-comers, together with the odd hours we have to keep in order to meet parishioners when they are free from work, it is not surprising that some clergy marriages fail. The irony in some cases is that the Church, or at least pastoral work with other people, is itself the 'other woman'. What other work could be more legitimate as a refuge from a difficult marriage, or a place to find personal space or fulfilment not granted by one's spouse? We can be awkward characters to live with too! Most dioceses have some form of counselling available for when a breakdown is feared. They are also more conscious than they once were of the need to treat an ex-spouse justly, given that there is no housing within the common fund of property that is divided between the spouses.

Another risk is that clerics may be seen as rivals by a suspicious spouse – and treated as co-respondents – because they offer a sympathetic ear to someone whose marriage is under strain. An awareness of this, and of the simple human fact of temptation, is important. Compston and many others in their time have warned against incautious counselling of members of the opposite sex alone. Judicious use of other clergy or bishops as a support team who are aware of a particularly delicate counselling situation or possible accusations (in the way that a Senior supervises the work of social workers) may be of help.

Clergy also have a symbolic role in living out Christian morality as surrogates for a less moral populace. There is also the specific instruction for elders, deacons and deaconesses in the Pastoral epistles that they should be monogamous. Not surprisingly, therefore, the remarriage of divorced clerics while they continue to exercise their ministry, or the ordination of a divorcee, raises some moral eyebrows. Some will argue that it betrays Christian standards. Others will shout 'discrimination', and point out that only divorced clerics will really understand the personal problems faced by other divorcees in their parishes and thus bring an added sympathy to their work. There is some truth in this, though logically such an argument means that no married cleric can minister to the single, and no young person to the elderly. A willingness to listen carefully is as important as direct experience.

Where remarried clerics continue to exercise their ministry, the matters to take into account are the privacy of all the parties involved, the confidence they have in the way the Church handles their case, and the trust of the Christian and wider public that Christian morals are not being undermined. When the ordination of divorcees was discussed the Archbishop made it clear that such care was intended. It may also be a situation in which Christian grace and forgiveness can be brought into clear public focus. Those whom it concerns, who are initially the congregation or other group with whom they work but may extend to the media, need to be reassured that they have worked through the causes and hurts of the divorce and done what is possible to correct their errors. However, they should not expect to know the details, both for the cleric's and the ex-spouse's sakes. Clergy need to have confidence in their Bishop and to discuss their work face to face with him or her[13], even if more detailed counselling is handled by someone with specialist expertise. Perhaps the credibility of the Church would be enhanced if the fact (rather than details) of such supportive counselling were made known, or even if some form of specific service of penance were known to have taken place. Again, details are not for public consumption nor that of the prurient press, but the knowledge that broken marriages are taken seriously affirms both Christ's forgiving grace and his ideals. It might also be appropriate at such services for the warden of the vicar's previous church, for example, to say on behalf of their congregation that unrealistic demands on his time or family had contributed to the breakdown, and on their behalf to ask God's forgiveness and grace to seek amendment of life.[14]

The way ahead

The bishops are considering divorce and remarriage as I write, while the Lord Chancellor published the Government's proposals in a White Paper, *Looking to the Future*, in April 1995 (London: HMSO, Cm 2799). This may date my suggestions even before they are printed.

I believe that Church policy on remarriage should not focus primarily on the past. It is right that the fulfilment of responsibilities from the past, especially those towards children, should be upheld, as was stressed in the General Synod debate. It is also important that the Church should not be seen to reward a couple whose adultery with each other was the cause of the demise of the first marriage. With those caveats, however, the main emphasis should be on support to make the new relationship work. The purgatory of the first marriage will not be redeemed or resurrected by allowing the second one to be a hell. Effort should go not into panels of assessors who will judge whether to allow the church service, but into a counselling service for couples who seek remarriage. Similarly, there should be training for the parish clergy who will make such preparations, and who perhaps should only be licensed to take second marriages after such training. For the couple this counselling should not be a hoop to jump through, but a means of hope for the future in the face of a redivorce rate twice that for first-time divorces. Counselling should look at the problem areas touched on in Chapter 6: responsible arrangements for existing children, and the pitfalls of step-parenting; throw-backs to past hurts; faults which may have led to the first breakdown; financial problems; and general marriage enrichment. Within the marriage services, post-ASB, the introduction should stress the healing purpose of marriage for people who come with a history of relationships (in or out of wedlock), and new prayers might cater for that reality. On the wider level, the Church should be prepared to campaign to see the conciliation services and voluntary relationship-guidance agencies adequately funded, and for the possibility of reconciliation to be kept to the fore, as the Lord Chancellor intends.

The Government's White Paper follows the lines of its Green Paper already discussed in this book. It proposes that divorce be granted one year after proceedings have been initiated so long as the couple have gone through mediation or by other means made proper arrangements for their children and other responsibilities, and in doing so have confirmed that their marriage cannot be salvaged. This removes the concept of fault, and the associated increase in conflict, from the *legal* process. If these proposals remove escalating accusations and counter-accusations and make reconciliation less difficult, so much the better. However in Christian moral terms, anger, blame and guilt will still remain in many cases (as the White Paper recognizes, paragraph 5. 21), calling for repentance and forgiveness. Those who claim that the Bible only allows divorce (and the possibility of remarriage) when the other party is guilty of some marital offence are mistaken, for they have missed the subtlety of Jesus' teaching, in which he exposed the moral responsibility even of the legally 'innocent' party.

It would appear that the conciliation service, which will brief people about the practical and emotional costs of divorce and guide their negotiations, will not be managed by existing court and Legal Aid administrators, and delivery of the service will be contracted out to existing or new mediation agencies (paragraph 7. 20). The proposals recognize that this will need to be piloted (paragraphs 7. 39–41) and that more mediators will need to be trained and standards set. It is clear that unless the Government plans a similar fiasco to that created in the early years of the Child Support Agency (when too much was demanded by so many of too few) the establishment of divorce through mediation will be a long, drawn-out process. Court officers are already overloaded as their work is restructured. Mediation and marriage-guidance services may find their workload increasing by fifteen times – a burden they cannot successfully take on overnight, even if trained counsellors were clamouring at their doors.

It is intended that the costs of the new system should not exceed those of the present adversarial system as funded by Legal Aid (£332 million in 1993–9, paragraph 6.2). The White Paper cites experience in Australia and America that mediation is cost-effective (paragraph 5.20) but does not offer evidence as to whether it leads to a drop in the actual rate of divorce. There should be a drop in the first year of the scheme, simply because what used to be dealt with by many couples in three to six months will now take a full year and more. No new grounds for divorce are added so the scheme might be deemed successful if the divorce rate rises at no more that its present 1 per cent per annum thereafter.

Perhaps the true test of its success will be if problems of health, and in children's education and behaviour, are found to decline as acrimony is reduced. Divorce will never be easy, never painless, and rarely the 'first-best' option. However we need to acknowledge that it is a fact in our culture and that the victims may need support and understanding for some time to come.

Notes

1. I refer to *Patterns for Worship*, (London: C.I.O., 1989), pp. 149f., the original consultative report to General Synod by the Liturgical Commission (GS898). Some of this material was published 'officially' in July 1995, as *Patterns for Worship!* (London: Church House Publishing).
2. If a church should feel that a strong disciplinary line is appropriate with regard to baptism, over who leads prayers or may receive communion (as was common practice in the 1950s), such a line should also be taken with other morally ambiguous situations, for instance, the bank manager whose branch has just foreclosed on the mortgage of a broken family, or workers whose perks delay council house repairs and so add to tensions in a marriage.
3. Cf. O. M. T. O'Donovan, *Liturgy and Ethics* (Nottingham: Grove Books, 1993), pp. 9f., discussing the American Episcopalian baptism service. The English service is somewhat thin.

4. Christopher Compston, *Recovering from Divorce* (London: Hodder and Stoughton, 1993), p. 96.
5. Andrew Cornes, *Divorce and Remarriage* (London: Hodder and Stoughton, 1994), p. 382.
6. Compston, *op. cit.*, pp. 127–42. Compston himself became a Christian while in the throes of a divorce, see p. 11.
7. Such as that prepared by CPAS (*One to One*), which does not, if I recall rightly, refer to the issue of remarriage, but does raise some of the key areas where communication is vital, such as feelings and finance, as well as faith.
8. Gavin Wakefield, *Where are the Men?* (Nottingham: Grove Books, 1988).
9. See P. Mansfield and J. Collard, *Beginning the Rest of Your Life* (London: One Plus One, 1988). The address of One Plus One is 12 New Burlington Street, London W1X 1FF. A booklet, *Step Carefully, preparation for marriages where there are children from a previous relationship* (London: Methodist Church Division of Education and Youth, n.d., 1995), has been prepared for those involved in preparing people for marriage by members of FLAME – Family Life and Marriage Enhancement.
10. Walter Trobisch, in *I Married You* (Leicester: InterVarsity Press).
11. *Marriage and the Standing Committee's Task* (London: Church Information Office, 1983), para. 41 of GS Misc. 180A.
12. O'Donovan, *op. cit.*, pp. 16f.
13. In a recent case in East Anglia a major bone of contention seems to have been that the bishop in question did not meet the clergyman or his proposed wife, or weigh the circumstances at a personal level, but left a junior member of the diocesan staff to communicate the bad news. Reported in *The Times*, 24 November 1994.
14. See O'Donovan, *op. cit.*

APPENDIX I

Henry VIII's Divorces

Henry VIII's role in the Anglican Church and his record of remarriage is raised, as a debating point if not a serious argument, when Anglican attitudes are discussed. Those who cite him range from his own collateral descendant, the Prince of Wales, through the couple who want a wedding in church to the pub debater. The argument is that a Church which owes its origin to its founder's desire for a divorce can hardly object if its members follow suit.

Henry VIII's influence over the corporate culture of the church, which he nationalized and stripped of its assets, was limited. Its characteristic features, such as the open Bible and worship in language 'understanded of the people', were not introduced until his closing years and were shaped in the reign of his son and younger daughter. His divorces provided the political circumstances within which the English Reformation began, but he is hardly an exemplar for Anglican practice.

Henry VIII's first divorce does not offer a precedent for anyone except a mediaeval monarch. Precedent is not morally binding. No community is committed to an action by precedent or past compromise if there are moral reasons for repudiating it. Repentance is part of the Christian message. A Church is free to admit, 'Our origins were compromised, but we will go forward from where we are with greater integrity.' An individual may say, 'I sinned, but will move on in the right ways from where I have landed myself.'

Within living memory England had been embroiled in civil war, which Henry VII resolved by an astute marriage. There remained the need for a male heir strong enough at Henry VIII's death to hold together the kingdom. Previously international considerations had prompted Henry VII to arrange another dynastic marriage, between his elder son Arthur and the daughter of the King of Spain, Catherine of Aragon, but Arthur died without issue and the alliance was threatened. The obvious remedy was for Catherine to marry the new heir, Henry. However this breached laws about forbidden degrees in marriage: a man might not marry his brother's wife. Marriage was a matter for canon law and the Pope was asked for dispensation for Henry to marry Catherine. This was granted and eventually the marriage took place.

The bride was considerably older than the groom. After a string of miscarriages and peri-natal deaths the needed male heir was not forthcoming. Only a daughter, Mary, survived infancy. By the early 1520s Catherine's age and the repeated child-deaths made the dynastic situation serious. Henry argued that the repeated deaths of his children were a sign of divine displeasure because his marriage was in fact incestuous. Whether his conscience was genuinely troubled or whether this was the best argument in order to be free to remarry is a matter for historians. Henry's tactics were, however, within the mediaeval tradition of dissolving inconvenient dynastic marriages on grounds of nullity. His 'divorce' from Catherine of Aragon was not a divorce in modern terms, but an annulment. Catherine's counter-arguments were also based within that school. She claimed that her marriage with Arthur (when both were young – he died at sixteen) was never consummated and should be disregarded. She had never really been Henry's brother's wife, so her marriage with Henry was valid.

Two factors complicated the question. Since papal dispensation had been granted for Henry and Catherine to marry, the new Pope could hardly declare that marriage void on the grounds that a previous Pope was wrong. Furthermore, Continental wars now meant that Catherine's nephew held military power over the Vatican. This discouraged the Pope from deciding against Catherine. He vacillated as long as he could until Henry declared independence anyway and found an Archbishop of Canterbury who accepted his arguments. He treated Catherine with some decency after the separation, according her the title Dowager Princess, and arranging for a pension for her.

Of his other marriages, only one ended in 'divorce' (with Anne of Cleves). Here too his arguments were based on what we might call nullity – this time his lack of proper consent. Such arguments would not sway a modern English court, which presumes that someone means what he said at the time of marriage, rather than accepting what he says he remembers he felt! The marriages with Anne Boleyn and Catherine Howard might in modern terms have been ended by divorce on the grounds of adultery. Henry treated their adultery as treason, with execution the means to their end – a procedure not available except to mediaeval monarchs. Thus Henry is not a good precedent, even in the possible case of princes of the realm.

APPENDIX II

Prayers about Marriage and Divorce

A litany is perhaps the most comprehensive way of praying for a complex issue, in which there are different opinions morally and different experiences of life. What follows is an attempt to pray realistically about the issues of marriage and divorce. It is intended as a model, not the definitive prayer on the subject.

Each bidding invites a response, such as:

Lord in your mercy . . . **hear our prayer.**

or

Father of all, . . . **hear your children's prayer.**

We thank you, Lord, for those who find in their marriage companionship and support, joy and delight,
and pray for those planning and preparing to be married *in this church or from this parish*.

We thank you for all that is rich and good in stable human love, yet pray for those whose loving relationships lack the security and commitment of marriage.

We thank you for the virtues of loyalty and trust, of repentance and forgiveness,
and pray for those who find loyalty a strain and forgiveness a hardship in their marriage,
or who know the hurt of loyalty betrayed and forgiveness abused.

We thank you for your love and support, care and understanding, in all circumstances of our lives,
and pray for your restoring power in the lives of adults and

children marred by desertion or divorce.

We thank you for the richness and joy in life that can come from our wider families,
and pray for those saddened because they lose out on the love of grandparents or grandchildren, cousins or aunts, because of the break-up of their immediate family.

We thank you for your insight and healing grace;
give us grace to see ourselves as you see us and as others see us, to understand our sins and faults,
to have confidence in the virtues and strengths you have given us,
and the wisdom and courage to repent of what has been wrong and to pursue what is wholesome.

We thank you that you know our hopes and fears, needs and duties, in all states and stages of life; you made us in your image; you shared our likeness as you lived among us.
Show us how to imitate you and reflect your character within our present state – married, single, widowed or divorced – for you are our pattern and our redeemer.

We thank you, Lord, that you are our Immanuel, God-with-us in our lives;
guide and strengthen us by your Spirit's presence in better or worse, richer or poorer, sickness or health, loneliness or companionship.

So, Lord, by our prayers and in your Spirit unite our wishes with your will,
    our living with your laws,
    our caring with your compassion,
    and our lives with your eternal love.
        for your mercy's sake. **Amen.**

At a second marriage
Almighty Father,
who alone know the forces which mould and mar our life and our loves;
forgive us for what has been wrong in our pasts,
>   heal the hurts which scar our memories,
>   help us to correct the failings of our present lives,
>   and direct and enrich our future,
>   through Jesus Christ our Saviour. **Amen.**

A suggested addition to the introduction of the (§6) ASB marriage service
For use at any wedding. It explains the jargon 'means of his grace' earlier in the clause and reflects points made earlier in this book.

'It is God's purpose that . . . they shall be united in that love as Christ is united with his Church,' *and that their love, given and received, should be a source of healing from hurts past and present, a defence against temptation, and a means of growth in faith and human understanding.*